Women Leadership and Empowerment

Women Leadership and Empowerment

By

Ramandeep Kour
Assistant Professor, Department of Commerce,
Cluster University of Jammu, Jammu

New Century Publications
New Delhi, India

NEW CENTURY PUBLICATIONS
4800 / 24, Bharat Ram Road,
Ansari Road, Daryaganj,
New Delhi - 110 002 (India)

Tel.: 011-2324 7798, 4358 7398, 4101 7798
E-mail: info@newcenturypublications.com

www.newcenturypublications.com

Editorial office:
LG – 7, Aakarshan Bhawan,
4754-57/23, Ansari Road, Daryaganj,
New Delhi – 110 002

Tel.: 011-4356 0919

First Published: **2019**

ISBN: **978-81-7708-486-3**

Published by New Century Publications and printed at Milan Enterprises, New Delhi.

Designs: Patch Creative Unit, New Delhi.

PRINTED IN INDIA

About the Book

Organizations are increasingly relying on women leaders because of their inherent and valuable attributes of nurturing, caring, self-sacrificing and emotional intelligence. India is one of the leading countries witnessing an increased participation of women employees at administrative and managerial positions. Women leaders are found to be efficient in decision-making in terms of providing reward and recognition to employees.

The realization of the goals of women leadership needs to be supported by the allocation of necessary human and financial resources to ensure gender equality at the local, regional, national, and international levels as well as by enhanced and increased international cooperation.

Empowerment of women has been a leading objective of state policy ever since the attainment of Independence in 1947. Gender equality is a constituent of development as well as an instrument of development. No country can be deemed developed if half of its population is severely disadvantaged in terms of basic needs, livelihood options, access to knowledge, and political voice. It is an instrument of development because without gender equality other goals of development will be difficult to achieve.

Effective and co-ordinated plans and programmes for full implementation of women-oriented policies require a clear research-based knowledge of ground realities of the socio-economic status of women, particularly the rural women.

The present work explains and examines in detail the issues related to leadership behaviour and styles of women. It also focuses on various aspects of policies and strategies to enhance economic, social and political empowerment of women.

About the Author

Dr. Ramandeep Kour is presently Assistant Professor in the Department of Commerce, Cluster University of Jammu, Jammu. She received her M.Com., M.Phil. and Ph.D. degrees from University of Jammu, Jammu. Specializing in the area of human resources development and management, she has published a number of research papers in reputed academic journals. She has participated and presented papers at various national and international conferences/seminars.

Contents

Preface

Gender equality is a constituent of development as well as an instrument of development. No country can be deemed developed if half of its population is severely disadvantaged in terms of basic needs, livelihood options, access to knowledge, and political voice. It is an instrument of development because without gender equality other goals of development will also be difficult to achieve.

Organizations are increasingly relying on women leaders because of their inherent and valuable attributes of nurturing, caring, self-sacrificing and emotional intelligence. India is one of the leading countries witnessing an increased participation of women employees at administrative and managerial positions. Women leaders are found to be efficient in decision-making in terms of providing reward and recognition to employees.

Programme support to enhance women's opportunities, potentials and activities need to have a dual focus: on the one hand, programmes aimed at meeting the basic as well as the specific needs of women for capacity building, organizational development and empowerment; and on the other, gender mainstreaming in all programme formulation and implementation activities. It is particularly important to expand into new areas of programming to advance gender equality in response to current challenges.

Advancement and empowerment of women has been a leading objective of state policy ever since the attainment of Independence in 1947. Women's lack of economic empowerment not only impedes growth and poverty reduction, but also has a host of other negative impacts including less favourable education and health outcomes for children. Thus, it is extremely important to ensure that women are economically, socially and politically empowered.

Effective and coordinated plans and programmes for the full implementation of women-oriented policies require a clear research-based knowledge of ground realities regards the socio-economic status of women, particularly rural women.

The realization of the goals of women empowerment needs to be supported by the allocation of necessary human and financial resources for specific and targeted activities to ensure gender equality at the local, regional, national, and international level as well as by enhanced and increased international cooperation.

Strong national machineries for the advancement of women and promotion of gender equality require political commitment at the highest level. Reforms to meet the challenges of the changing world are essential to ensure women's equal access to institutions and organizations. Institutional and conceptual changes are a strategic and important aspect of creating an enabling environment for the implementation of policies and programmes for the advancement of women.

Acknowledgements

First of all, I express my gratitude to the Almighty for giving me strength and determination to pursue my academic ambitions.

I take this opportunity to place on record my deep sense of gratefulness to Professor Neetu Andotra for her continuous support and encouragement to accomplish my goals.

Thanks are also due to my family members for their moral support and understanding, in particular my loving parents, parents-in-law, husband Mr. Prabjeet Singh and daughter Eknoor.

Jammu **Ramandeep Kour**

1

Women Leadership Behaviour and Styles

Leadership behaviour is an art, skill, attribute and a characteristic used by a manager in different situations in accordance with individual and organisational values. Women leadership behaviour which comprises of communication, motivational ability, emotional intelligence, decision-making, and cooperative attitude may boost employees' satisfaction, trust and respect and avoid employee absenteeism and turnover.

1.1 Leadership among Women

The era of economic reforms and consistently high economic growth rate for several years has created more employment opportunities in general for men and women in particular, in the corporate sector. Traditionally, the senior management positions in corporate sector in India were occupied by men, but that scenario has been gradually undergoing a change in recent years.

Leadership among women is an emerging reality and organisations are now focusing on women leadership. Despite this positive evolution, the number of female leaders is surprisingly low. In the European Union, women hold only 11 percent of the top executive positions and account for only 4 percent of the CEOs and presidents of boards of directors. In the United States, women have entered into the paid labour force in large numbers and now constitute almost 58 percent of workforce. In India, the percentage of women in senior positions in various sectors has risen to 14 percent.

Women tend to work better in complexity, are better listeners, emotionally intelligent and make a significant impact on different organisations by using their own style of leadership. There seems to be a shift in the new management era towards more feminine styles of leadership emphasising connectedness and collaboration in public leadership, including highly visible positions. Women attributes like self-sacrificing, being empathetic, sensitive, compassionate, cooperative and accommodative are increasingly associated with effective administration. While these characteristics are inherent and valuable, women possessing the attributes of a good leader still face higher attrition and slower career mobility. Women have been making a significant impact in all segments of the economy such as education, culture, insurance and banking.

1.2 Women Leadership Behaviour: Conceptual Framework

Leadership is a process of interaction between leaders and followers where the leader attempts to influence followers to achieve a common goal. Leadership is mainly associated with group activity and group processes that raises the level of human conduct and ethical aspiration of both the leader and the employee. A leader not only commits his employee to organisational goals, but also pool needed resources, guides and motivate subordinates to reach the goals and has a direct influence on the success or failure of an organisation. Leadership behaviour is defined as series of attitudes, characteristics and skills used by a manager in different situations in accordance with individual and organisational values.

Leadership behaviour among women has significant impact on employees' job satisfaction and organisational commitment levels in various service sectors. The cooperative attitude, communication skills, motivating ability and emotional intelligence among women managers assists subordinates to enhance their job performance by overcoming stress and conflicts. The successful performance of employees in service sector depends on effective leadership behaviour of women with regard to employee development, open communication and the integration of individual goals with the organisational goals.

1.2.1 Dimensions of Women Leadership Behaviour: Women leadership behaviour influences employees' work efforts and transforms the system of performing job in service organisations. The dimensions of women leadership behaviour towards employees in service organisational setting are as under:

A. Emotional Intelligence: Emotional intelligence is defined as the capacity of an individual to understand the emotions of one self and others. It is mainly concerned with the behavioural dispositions and self-perceived capabilities to understand other's emotions. There is a comprehensive coverage of emotional intelligence factors like personality, self-control, emotionality, sociability and well-being. Female leaders are found to be rated higher than male leaders on measures of emotional and social intelligence.

B. Communication: Communication is the transmission of information from one person to another or too many people, whether verbally or non-verbally. It is a vital part of human life and is also important in business, education and any other situation where people encounter each other. Good communication is always one of the most difficult skills to master and probably a great source of friction and conflict in any organisation. A leader employs full range of communication skills and resources to minimise interferences and to create and deliver messages that guide, direct, motivate or inspire others to action. Women communicate in a competent manner and show directness and initiative which lacks in men.

C. Motivation: Motivation is a driving force which urges a person to do or not to do something. Motivation can be regarded as the sum of effort which people are eager to put in their work and depend upon the degree to which they feel their emotional needs will be satisfied. On the other hand, employees' are de-motivated when they feel something in the organisation prevents them from attaining success.

D. Self-sacrificing: Self-sacrifice implies the willingness of an individual to bear the loss of personal welfare for maintaining personal belief, integrity and values. Subsequently, self-sacrificing women leaders will be more efficient and have the capability to influence their employees to achieve a higher level of performance than non self-sacrificing male leaders. Self-sacrificing attribute builds mutual trust, respect and follower acceptance as a role model that helps in making a women leader effective.

E. Decision-making: Decision-making is a very important day to day job of a leader when it is focussed on the resources, plans, mission and goals. Decision-making can be considered as an interaction between problem that needs to be solved and person who wishes to solve it within a specific environment. Decision-making ability, flexibility and perseverance were found to have significant influence on women leaders as they are stern and their decisions are not influenced by others.

F. Attitude: Attitude plays a central role in the formation of people's beliefs and behaviours. It refers to a general and enduring positive or negative feeling about some person, object or issue. Attitudes have two parts, which determines how they affect leadership, one being the effective component, the other being the behavioural component.

The first component is how someone feels about doing something, while the second is how they behave or act regarding how they feel about something. Leadership is affected by attitudes in the sense that a leaders' attitude about their subordinates affects their satisfaction and performance. Female leaders hold a more cooperative attitude than male leaders towards encouraging subordinates to prepare themselves professionally.

1.2.2 Employee Performance Outcomes of Women Leadership Behaviour: Leadership behaviour among women has significant effect on employee commitment and employee performance in various sectors. The capabilities, skills, behaviour, guidance and competency of women leaders influence employee performance which enables them to perform better and also help in maintaining healthy leader-member exchange relationships. The performance of an employee is assessed in terms of trust, job satisfaction, conflict and absenteeism which have been elaborated as under:

A. Trust: Trust is defined as the expectations, supposition or confidence in another's upcoming activities that will be beneficial and favourable in one's interest. Employee trust is the belief of an employee that arises within the organisation towards their leader which is based on commonly shared norms and mutual understanding. Moreover, trust of employees towards their respective leaders also influences the behaviour of employees at workplace, which in turn affects their satisfaction and performance.

B. Job Satisfaction: Job satisfaction is defined as the feeling that a worker has about his job and general attitude towards their work in a job and is influenced by the perception of one's job. It is the positive attitude or emotional disposition that people may gain from work or through aspects of work.

C. Employee Conflict: Employee conflict is mainly associated with the major difference in ideas, beliefs and viewpoints relating to work related issues. In general, it is believed that employee conflict at work place arises due to unfavourable decisions taken by leaders, and unhealthy interpersonal relationship among employees and executives.

D. Employee Absenteeism: Employees are the assets of every organisation and employee absenteeism is the practice or habit of being absent at the work place. Absenteeism is a situation when a person fails to come for work when he is scheduled to work. Absenteeism does not indicate the physical inexistence of an employee but also signifies the mental absence of the employees faced by the organisations in a modern world that has resulted in employee turnover.

1.3 Women Leadership Styles

Leadership style in an organisation is regarded as a prerequisite that plays a significant role in enhancing the interest and performance of individuals in an organisation. Leadership styles can be conceptualised as a composition of three elements viz., personality, behaviour and action of the leaders. Leadership styles are patterns of behaviour, governance and supervision which a leader usually adopts in enhancing the performance of his/her employees. Women leaders develop and adopt different leadership styles as per their personality, qualification, training and experience in accordance with the situation encountered for maintaining a healthy working relationship with employees that in turn enhances employee satisfaction and their performance.

1.3.1 Dimensions of Women Leadership Styles: Women leaders in different situations adopt different leadership styles to balance the interest of their employees and team members for achieving organisational objectives. Various leadership styles adopted by women in service organisations are discussed in detail as under:

A. Autocratic Style: Autocratic style is also known as authoritarian leadership style in which leaders give orders to their employees without explanation of the reasons and expect instant obedience without any argument. This style is vested with the power to make decisions and policies alone by the leader and the instructions the employees receive as to what they want them to do and how they should do it without getting any advice from the subordinates.

B. Democratic Style: Democratic style involves the redistribution of power and authority between employees and managers to encourage employee involvement in decision-making process. This style is also known as participative style in which a leader helps, assists and provides guidance to the employees while performing various tasks within the organisation. Moreover, it is generally associated with consensus, consultation, delegation and involvement of employees.

C. Laissez-faire Style: The laissez-faire leadership style is also known as the 'hands-off' style which is defined as the avoidance and absence of leadership. In this style, the manager provides little or no direction to employees and gives them freedom as much as possible to perform their work. The leader with this style allows the employees to make decision, but the leader is mainly responsible for the decisions that are made. This style of leadership is used when employees are able to analyse the situation and determine what needs to be done and how to do it. Leader with this style gives no continuous feedback or supervision and avoids active participation of employees in making major decisions.

D. Transformational Style: Transformational leadership is defined as a leadership approach that causes change in individuals and social systems and stimulate employees to see problems in new ways and help them to harness their full potential. It implies a leader's ability to translate ethical values and motivate employees to inspire a feeling of loyalty and trust. Moreover, it is a combination of factors like idealised influence, inspirational motivation, intellectual stimulation and individualised consideration and focus towards changing the future by nurturing the performance of employees to the maximum of their potential.

E. Transactional Style: Transactional style is also known as managerial leadership in which the leader promotes compliance of his followers both through reward and punishment. It depends strongly on the leader's power to reinforce subordinates for the successful completion of tasks. Transactional leaders have three primary characteristics. First, transactional leaders work with their team members and try to get a reward for their goals. Second, they will exchange the rewards and promises of the reward for work efforts. Finally, they are responsive to the immediate self-interests of workers. Transactional leadership can be related with three different approaches, namely: (i) contingent reward in which leaders clarify the employee work that must be achieved and rewarded, (ii) management by exception (passive) where the leaders intervene only when problem arise and (iii) management by exception (active) in which leaders actively monitor the work of employees.

1.4 Employee Satisfaction and Performance

Employee satisfaction is used to describe whether the employees are happy, contended and are fulfilling their desires and needs at work. It may be defined as a positive emotional response from the assessment of a job or specific aspects of a job and is influenced by various factors namely, working conditions, supervision, policy and administration, advancement, compensation, interpersonal relationships, recognition and empowerment which affects their performance. Employee satisfaction is a more comprehensive term that comprises of satisfaction among employees with their job, leaders, work environment etc.

Employee performance signifies the quality, knowledge, capability and the creativeness of an employee towards the accomplishment of the work in line with the responsibility and duties assigned by the leaders during the specific period of time. It is related to performance outcome or contribution of employee to achieve their goals with respect to the assessment of standard parameters. Employee performance can also be conceptualised as a process of quantifying the efficiency and effectiveness of employee actions. In service organisations, employee performance is embraced by evaluating employee proficiency, execution of assigned duties and responsibilities, meeting deadlines, work efficiency and employee productivity that leads to an effective feedback and good organisational relations.

1.5 Women Leadership: Barriers and Challenges

In a modern competitive and dynamic business world, women constitute around half of the total workforce in services sector and play an important role in augmenting the pace of economic growth. However, women experience diverse barriers and challenges in leadership positions, which are discussed as under:

1.5.1 Balance between Work and Family: There are several possible factors that become pitfalls for women on the path of leadership. Firstly, the impact of family responsibilities on a women's career is increasingly growing as men do not fully share domestic responsibilities. Women are putting their best efforts to trade off the work responsibilities between family and career. Secondly, women while facing this balance are bent upon to take more leaves, maternity breaks and less working hours.

1.5.2 Lack of Confidence: Generally, men are characterised as more confident than women especially regarding financial and complex decisions. Low confidence among women is evident from the fact that business women generally report lower level of business profitability in all terms.

1.5.3 Women Leadership Identity: The role of the leader is process-oriented which serves as an identity for the person who internalises through feedback of employees and past experiences. Indian culture emulates that people have a stereotype notion regarding women leaders as not being decisive, assertive and independent whereas they do possess a friendly and caring attitude and a selfless attribute. This gender bias interferes with the growth development of women leaders.

1.5.4 Role Model: Female leaders are not considered to be good role models from an employee's perspective. Women tend to use communication skills and behaviour strategies that have worked for them based on their past experience whereas men normally imitate strategies used by their seniors and yet role modelling is not instinctive in women.

1.5.5 Career Paths: Women are more likely to have non-linear career paths, spending more time with the family or generally avoiding the jobs involving out-of-town travelling. As women climb the ladder of career growth, the responsibilities will become more imperative and demanding and they may face lesser flexibility across all regions which may create obstacles in their career path.

1.5.6 Networks, Mentors and Sponsors: The next challenge faced by women leaders is the limited access to the networks and sponsors which are essential for the success of women leaders. Women leaders are reluctant towards networking as they perceive it to be inauthentic and treat it like an obligation to involve in stereotypical masculine and networking strategy.

1.5.7 Glass Ceiling: The term 'glass ceiling' means

invisible artificial barriers within the hierarchy that restrain deserving women to reach at the top level of management. It is related with the feature of invisible and transparent layer that reflects informal rules and regulations to block the development of women in an organisation.

1.5.8 Resistance to Female Leadership: The next possible barrier for female leaders is that there is a direct effect of the unconscious use of gender stereotypes. Male employees develop a tendency towards resisting women leaders which is based on their gender stereotype notion. This confrontation is because of two stereotype beliefs i.e. gender symbolism and gender stereotypes.

1.5.9 Selection Process: In spite of a large pool of qualified and experienced women employees, companies do not consider them for suitable promotions. Further, another rationale is that the existing top management positions are held by men who tend to promote other male employees who share a similar attitude and thus avoid the scope of promotion of female employees at higher management positions.

1.6 Leadership among Women in the Indian Context

Women constitute half of world's population, receive one-tenth of the world's total income, account for two-thirds of the world's working hours and are owners of only one-hundredth of the immovable properties globally. Women are at the heart of development process and participation of women in economic activities is essential not only for the individual development but also for the prosperity of households as well as for the economy as a whole. The process of industrialisation, urbanisation and the increased educational and employment opportunities for women have brought about drastic changes in the traditional attitudes and values of urban women in India.

In 2015, a total of 586 million women were contributing to the progress of the economy by engaging themselves in direct and allied agricultural activities, running small shops, selling by-products or handicraft products, engaging in community services, etc. Globally, the share of women as a contributor to family income has decreased significantly by 17 percent over the last 20 years and to a lesser extent among men by 8.1 percent over the same period, resulting in a decrease in the income gender gap from 19.5 percent in 1995 to 10.6 percent in 2015. This trend is a part of an economic restructuring which impelled a shift among women from agricultural sector to service sectors like education, health care, banking, insurance, etc. Women hold 43 percent of the top executive positions and account for only 24 percent of the CEOs, presidents and board of directors, which surprisingly is increasing.

In India, 70 percent of the women are contributing to the economy through their active participation in different service sectors. Traditionally, the Indian culture hindered women's access to jobs in public and private sector, factories, stores and outlets, but that scenario has been gradually changing.

The Women Reservation Policy (1974) was framed to give the right to women for their representation in the Panchayati Raj system, as a sign of political empowerment. This bill also envisaged provisions for encouraging women to place themselves in a position of respect and prestige. According to the Economic Times Survey (2015), 33 percent women held leadership position in the education sector, 24 percent in the banking sector, 17 percent in health care, 12 percent in the insurance sector and 14 percent in the corporate sector. This reveals that women have made substantial gains at workplace and the glass ceiling has been broken. Successful women leaders are coming forward and making a significant contribution by providing cross-industry mentoring for successor generations of women and providing equal opportunities to overcome prejudices against women abilities.

1.6.1 Women in Education Sector: Today, women actually outnumber men in college, have pulled ahead in pursuing master's degrees and have reached equal numbers in most doctoral and professional programs. But this high level of participation in education does not translate to comparably high representation in leadership roles in academia. Women still lag significantly behind men in status, salary and leadership positions. Women made up around 57 percent of the student population and received 60 percent of all degrees conferred in 2014-15. In 2015-16, women received 62 percent of associate degrees, 57 percent of bachelor's degrees, 61 percent of master's degrees, and 20 percent and 50 percent of doctoral and professional degrees respectively. Moreover, women account for 42 percent of the full-time faculty at degree granting institutions, up from 32 percent in 2014. While this represents a substantial progress, still women overall are underrepresented in quite a number of faculties. Today, women constitute 26 percent of full professors, 40 percent of associate professors, 47 percent of assistant professors and 53 percent of lecturers.

1.6.2 Women in the Banking Sector: The number of talented women with a finance background joining the banking sector has been increasing every year. Women constitute a little over 11 percent of the workforce in finance and banking industry. According to the Catalyst Census, 2013, women represented 17.6 percent of executives and 17.9 percent of the board of directors in the banking sector. In 2015, women represented 23.1 percent of all senior and managerial level positions in public and private sector banks.

1.6.3 Women in Health Sector: Women occupy 78 percent of the healthcare industry workforce and are the largest consumers of healthcare products. They remain underrepresented in top management and executive leadership positions and serious structural barriers appear to be impeding their progress towards greater gender diversity. The American College of Healthcare Executives (ACHE) conducted periodic surveys in 2006, 2009, 2012 and 2015 and found that 45 percent women executives are more likely to be a departmental head and 34 percent in other staff positions, whereas men are much more likely to be chief executive officers (CEOs), chief operating officers (COOs), presidents or vice-presidents.

1.6.4 Women in the Insurance Sector: Insurance often has the reputation for being a conservative industry typically dominated by men. However, in the cooperative and mutual insurance sector, women are taking up a much more significant role. Women are currently earning only 77 percent on every rupee earned by their male counterparts which decreases to just 62 percent when looking at the insurance industry. Only 6 percent of top insurance industry executive positions in India are held by women according to a report by St. Joseph's University. Globally, women make up only 12 percent of insurance industry board seats.

Women leadership behaviour that characterises and comprises of communication skills, motivational ability, emotional intelligence, and cooperative attitude has been instrumental in employee work motivation, employee trust and support, job satisfaction and reduction in conflict and absenteeism. Moreover, an effective women leader adopts suitable leadership style to meet the upcoming demands of the prevalent situation in which they work. Therefore, women leadership involves strategic integration of diverse leadership styles which results in efficient and effective management of subordinates, improved employee performance and organisational development.

2

Women and Leader-member Exchange Relationship (LMX)

LMX is a social exchange of psychological benefits between leaders and followers, which are characterised as being low- or high-quality, based on the extent of mutual trust, respect, liking and obligation between the two parties. Leader-member exchange (LMX) also describes the dyadic process in which roles and expectations are developed for a leader with each subordinate. The quality of the exchange relationship usually differs from one subordinate to another. High exchange relationships are developed with some employees, whereas low exchange relationships are likely to be developed with other employees. It is advocated that perceived similarities between the leader styles and the employee performance has led to higher quality leader-member exchange relationships.

2.1 Low Representation of Women

A number of reasons for low representation of women in leadership positions have been identified which include latent discrimination, male dominance, limited access, negative attitude from subordinates, inadequate family support, lack of awareness, fear of failure, job-family conflicts, lack of motivation, lack of confidence, low participation, low-risk taking ability and lack of competitiveness.

Women representation at the top level of management is proportionately very low as compared to men which act as a major barricade in propagating leadership among women.

Rapid modernisation processes have influenced employment opportunities and professional development for women in different sectors. Women leadership and decision-making is now the focal point of research as women acquire a multiplicity of talents, understanding, and communicative and social skills for their overall economic and social empowerment.

Women leaders develop and adopt different leadership styles as per their qualification, training and experience in order to sustain healthy leader-member exchange relationship, which enhances employee job satisfaction and employee performance.

Technology is emerging as an indispensable part of our work and social life, therefore, it is suggested that women leaders should be tech-savvy and should promote usage of technology to ease work processes and improve efficiency of the employees.

2.2 Leadership Style

Women cover a large segment of the managerial talent across globe, but their representation at top level positions in business and public administration is very low. The leadership prospect for women managers is a critical issue in gender equality and remains a researchable proposition. This chapter provides background information for clear understanding of different concepts and variables related to women leadership, issues pertaining to women representation and challenges faced by them in service sector in India.

Leadership style is considered as a major factor that has influenced the performance of organisations, managers and employees. Transactional leadership style appears to characterise leadership with strong masculine qualities, as it includes competitiveness, hierarchical authority, high control for the leader and analytical problem solving while women are equipped with the qualities of a transformational leader. Eagly and Johnson (2001) found that women are more democratic and participative whereas men are autocratic and directive. Participative leadership style among women is associated with increased feelings of empowerment and job satisfaction.

Laissez faire leadership style has significantly but negatively influenced employee satisfaction and employee performance. Leadership styles could differ with regards to personality and behaviour even though women and men are selected on the basis of same criteria and that women, owing to their social capabilities, can perform better in their managerial role than men.

2.3 Women Leadership Styles and LMX

LMX is a social exchange of psychological benefits between leaders and followers, based on the extent of common trust, reverence, liking and commitment between the two parties. It is positively correlated with composite measures of women leadership styles namely, transformational, transactional, participative, and *laissez faire*. LMX measures include mutual respect, trust and the overall quality of the working relationship which influences transformational leadership style. The transactional leadership dimensions namely, contingent rewards, and management by exception (passive and active) are found to be significant predictors of LMX. There exists a positive relation between participative style of leadership and LMX as participative leaders provide the opportunity to the subordinates with the necessary expertise and interest to improve the quality of a leader's decisions, thereby helping to justify a high-quality exchange relationship.

2.4 LMX and Employee Performance

Leader-member exchange relationship (LMX) describes the dyadic process by which roles and expectations are developed by a leader with each subordinate. The quality of the exchange relationship usually differs from one subordinate to another. High exchange relationships are developed with some employees, whereas lower exchange relationships are likely to be developed with other employees. LMX is positively correlated with subordinate performance. LMX theory asserted that high quality LMX relationships are characterized by high levels of trust, commitment and loyalty and contribute to elevated levels of member task performance. The relationship between LMX and employee performance is moderated by superior perceived organizational support. High LMX followers were rated consistently high on performance regardless of their objective, performance level and tenure with the leader.

Follower ratings of job performance will be highest when leader and follower perceptions of LMX are similar and positive and lowest when both the leader and the follower perceive the relationship less favourably.

Leader-member exchange relationship (LMX) describes the process by which roles and expectations are developed by a leader with each subordinate.

2.5 Motivation and Communication

Motivation plays a vital role in fostering strong team spirit among team members. Motivating ability and cooperative attitude of women managers helps subordinates to enhance their job performance which reduces stress and conflict. Further, motivation and demographic variables significantly contribute to the entrepreneurial intention among women and bring about distinct personality and motivational strengths in leadership. Decision-making power is identified as an important factor which influences women leadership behaviour, service quality and innovation. There is an opinion that decisions taken by women leaders are consultative in nature which improves workers' satisfaction, work environment, minimise employee absenteeism and attrition rate. Further, self-sacrifice as well as cooperative attitude of women leaders encourages mutual trust and respect, thereby reducing stress and enhancing job satisfaction among the employees.

Communication and interpersonal relationships are closely related to organisational factors that affect an employee's satisfaction and his/her performance, which leads to overall better performance in the organisations. Managers who communicate effectively with their subordinates are found to achieve better group decision-making and increased trust among employees.

A leader must have emotional intelligence in order to understand the emotions of others for developing better and healthy relationships at the workplace. Female leaders scored higher than male leaders regarding emotional and social intelligence, innovativeness, flexibility and perseverance. Women managers are found to be more emotionally intelligent to manage stress and conflict among subordinates leading to enhanced job satisfaction.

Leader-employee interactions have negative influence on employee satisfaction, manifest in stress, unwillingness to go to work, reduced productivity, and increased absenteeism and turnover. Employees' satisfaction with leader plays a crucial role in determining an employee performance. It may be defined as a positive emotional response from the assessment of a job or specific aspects of a job and is influenced by various factors namely, working conditions, supervision, policy and administration, advancement, compensation, interpersonal relationships, recognition and empowerment.

Performance can be conceptualised as a process of quantifying the efficiency and effectiveness of actions. Positive performance of satisfied employees is more productive for the organisations. Job satisfaction has a positive impact on employee performance as job satisfaction contributes to certain characteristics regards individual employee performance.

However, research studies have empirically proved that the existing relationships between women leadership style and leader-member exchange relationship (LMX) and employee satisfaction and employee performance are scanty.

In short, women across nations are adopting different leadership roles in the society and they might carry these roles and responsibilities in a different manner than men, which has drawn attention from academicians, managers and researchers. Moreover, successful leadership is related with the persuasive source of executive development and continuous realistic improvement for enhancing organisational performance.

Leadership styles are the patterns of behaviour used by women leaders in order to influence satisfaction and performance of employees working in different sectors. Women leaders adopt an assortment of leadership styles for maintaining quality relationship with their employees.

Women leadership provides supervision, direction and control in service organisations that helps employees to follow their leaders and achieve the desired goal of job satisfaction. Women leaders adopt appropriate proportions of various suitable leadership behaviour and styles in order to develop trust, confidence and high morale among employees which reduces employee conflict and absenteeism. For enhancing zeal and optimism among employees, women leaders should adopt the desired leadership style which is more conducive to the existing organisational culture.

Therefore, it is concluded that women leaders are efficient enough to manage their employees, to motivate them to perform better and encourage them to be more committed towards the organisational success.

Women leadership is the focus of activity through which the goals and objectives of the employees as well as the organisation are accomplished. Women leaders in different sectors combine various aspects or factors of leadership styles depending on the environmental turbulence or volatility, restrictiveness and technological sophistication, which ultimately influences satisfaction and performance among employees.

3

Women Leadership Behaviour and Conflict among Employees

Leader is a vital human resource that contributes actively for the development of an organisation and society at large. Perceived leadership attributes among women have a direct impact on subordinate satisfaction and performance. Stress and conflict is a timely and important topic issue for organisational leaders. Highly conflict and stress-laden workplaces present challenges to organisational leaders as they are faced with the task of managing the workforce while concurrently maintaining commitment and morale. Women leaders themselves can often be a central source of reducing stress and conflicts among the employees.

Leadership is an art, skill and knowledge of the leader to manage a group of people who gather under specific goals and prompts them to realise these goals. Women leadership in service sector plays an important role in accelerating the progress of economy and has opened new doors of opportunity for women at various administrative levels. Leadership behaviour of women has significant impact on employees' job satisfaction and organisational commitment.

Co-operative attitude, communication skills, motivating ability and self-sacrificing attribute in women managers helps subordinates to enhance their job performance by overcoming stress and conflicts and thereby achieving organisational goals. The present chapter provides us with a base to assess the impact of women leadership behaviour in reducing stress and conflict among employees.

3.1 Male and Female Employees

Male employees generally believe in masculine leadership

and accept them as leaders. LMX is not significant in relationship between male employees and female leaders, as they perceive women leaders as incompetent, less confident and less risk takers. Further, female employees prefer to work under female leaders as they feel comfortable to work with them.

Male and female employees are rated as equally satisfied with their working relationship with women leaders as female subordinates under female supervisors would perceive significantly more supervisory mentoring than their gender dyad combinations.

Female leaders are found to be more humane, emotionally intelligent, participative and higher on integrity, team-oriented and willing to make self-sacrifices as compared to male leaders.

It was found that women employees working in banks rated feminine leaders as high in the fields of communication, active listening, empathy, motivation, high-quality work and more sensitive to their co-workers' needs. Male employees prefer to work under male leaders as masculine leadership was found to be significant in terms of innovativeness, flexibility and perseverance.

In India, despite increase in women's education and involvement in the service sectors, representation of women in administrative jobs is significantly low as compared to men. The few women, who reach the executive level, make us believe that there is a dynamic change in the gender equations within the service organisations and businesses. Many studies have found a very gloomy outlook about women representation in executive jobs in India and explored the reasons and barriers that retard their advancement.

Women are more interpersonally oriented, more task-oriented, more democratic and more transformational than men in the health sector. It was found that female leaders in the banking sector form a unique one-to-one interpersonal relationship with their male and female subordinates by adopting democratic and transformational leadership styles. Women leaders differ in their behaviours and styles as they tend to work better in complexity, are better listeners and are considered to be more emotionally intelligent as compared to male leaders. But women leadership roles can differ in relation to their personality and behaviour even though women and men are selected in accordance with the situation encountered.

The quality of the supervisor-subordinate relationship is considered to be a vital resource for enhancing the effectiveness of an employee as well that of an organisation. Employee perception towards their leaders is based on the optimistic behaviour of leaders, which strengthens their working relationship. Male employees often prefer males as their perceived leader.

3.2 Women Leadership Behaviour and Absenteeism among Employees

Leaders are expected to achieve stability by reducing complexity through better planning and counselling, and solving problems using reductionist rather than holistic thinking which results in job satisfaction among the employees. An effective women leader recognises the importance of interactions, correlation and unpredictability among ensembles or aggregates of individuals. When leaders facilitate 'correlation' and 'interaction', they help others make sense out of what is happening, give meaning to unfolding events and facilitating one to one communication with the employees thereby bringing about increased employee retention and resultantly lower attrition rate. The ingrained peculiarities of female harbingers namely, motivational skills, communications skills, decision-making ability etc. helps to counsel their subservient to give effective organisational results by bringing in better performance.

3.3 Women Leadership Behaviour and Job Satisfaction among Employees

Women leadership behaviour has emerged as an important

topic as organisations attempt to build community resources, enlarge employee commitment, trust and improve knowledge-sharing among employees. Job satisfaction is regarded as an important component which implies one's feelings or state of mind regarding the nature of their work.

Employees with high job satisfaction are likely to exert more efforts in their assigned tasks and pursue organisational interests. There exists a positive and significant relationship between leadership behaviour among women and employees' job satisfaction. Interpersonal behaviour had positive effects on employees and organisational performance because good communication skills, motivational ability, cooperative attitude of a leader fosters and creates an understanding and builds confidence in employees in order to achieve their personal and organisational objectives. There is a positive relationship between behaviour of women leaders and satisfaction of their respective employees as effective leadership and employees' job satisfaction are two factors that have been regarded as fundamental to organisational success.

3.4 Women Leadership Behaviour and Trust among Employees

In today's comprehensive and complex organisations, leaders and their employees have increasingly diverse responsibilities and they generally work and perform their duties interdependently. Women leaders are important key players of every organisation and have to play an essential role in the attainment of organisational goals by creating a climate that would influence employee commitment, motivation, trust and their overall performance. However, attributes of women leaders like open communication, clear roles, effective listening, equitable assignments, diversity and self-assessment significantly and positively influences trust among employees. A number of studies have also examined the effects of communication skills, effective decision-making, motivational power, etc. on trust among employees.

Women occupy an important place in various sectors by balancing their duties and responsibilities at home and at workplace. Women leaders exceeded men on four transformational scales namely, idealised influence, inspirational motivation, intellectual stimulation and individualised consideration in the education sector.

A more participative organisational culture provides better opportunities for women in telecommunication sector and female leaders are perceived to be more participative and humane. There exist no significant differences between male and female leaders regarding *laissez faire* style. In healthcare sector, women leaders adopt transformational leadership scales namely, idealised influence, inspirational motivation, intellectual stimulation and individualised consideration.

3.5 Women Leadership Styles and Satisfaction of Employees

Leadership is considered as a major factor that influences the performance of organisations, managers and employees. The quality of the leader-employee relationship has a great influence on an employee's self-esteem and employee satisfaction. Employees' satisfaction occurs when employees are fully committed and happy with their work and leaders who fulfil their desire at work place. Transformational style as compared to transactional and *laissez faire* style has a stronger and positive effect on employee attitudes towards their job and job environment which ultimately affects employees work performance. This leadership style also raises employees' awareness about their need to grow, validates their self-expression and motivates them to perform at new and higher levels.

Participative style will be more effective than other styles to obtain employee's job satisfaction and show more concern for employees' problems at work. The autocratic style leads to lower levels of job satisfaction among employees, while democratic style leads to a higher level of job satisfaction.

Laissez faire style is not positively related to indicators of leadership effectiveness such as employee satisfaction, motivation and performance. Various studies have provided us with valuable insights into the impact of various women leadership styles as regards the satisfaction of employees.

Employee satisfaction plays an imperative role in influencing employee performance. Employee satisfaction implies a positive emotional response from the assessment of a job or specific aspects of a job and is influenced by various factors namely, working conditions, supervision, policy and administration, advancement, compensation, interpersonal relationships, recognition and empowerment which ultimately affects their performance.

Employee satisfaction has a positive effect on employees' job performance, which in turn shows more productive results for an organisation. There is a positive relation between satisfied employees and their performance, as positive performance of the satisfied employees is quite valuable for an organisation than the less satisfied employees.

Many studies have focused on factors namely, individual factor, societal factor and organisational factor that act as encumbrance in the growth of women leadership and recommend strategies to overcome such barriers.

3.6 Women and the Services Sector

Women leadership behaviour comprising of communication, motivational ability, emotional intelligence, decision-making, attitude and self-sacrificing potency may boost employee satisfaction, work environment, trust and respect and avoid employee absenteeism. Cooperative attitude, communication skills, motivating ability and emotional intelligence among women managers assists subordinates to enhance their job performance by overcoming stress. The successful performance of employees in service sector depends on effective leadership behaviour of women with regard to employee development, open communication and the integration of individual goals with the organisational goals.

Service sector plays an indispensable role in accelerating economic growth and development across all countries. The growth of the service sector and its contribution to income and employment generation are the indices of progress. Service organisations have provided a tremendous source of employment for many women in recent years but its significance and representation within the service industry varies across different places in almost all countries of the world. Women are more sincere, emotionally intelligent, bright, enthusiastic and able to perform diverse roles in all business spheres. In the present era, women are attaining equal importance as men in the business world and are also sharing major positions in the top level management of the service sector.

As representation of women leaders in the total workforce is quite noticeable, gender disparity among senior and junior staff members has also shrunk, right from the factory floor to fighter planes and from hospitals to banks. Empirically, it has been found that women working at the top level in an organisation significantly influence employee satisfaction, employee commitment, employee absenteeism, employee trust and employee performance. Therefore, it is imperative to recognise the role of diverse styles and behaviour adopted by women leaders in select service sectors namely, education, banking, heath care and insurance.

4

Women Empowerment and Development

Social health of any community depends, to a great deal, upon the status, functions and responsibilities of the women in the family and in the community. Social conditions should help create opportunities for women for creative self-expression, so that they can make their full contribution towards the economic and social life of the community. Some problems of women have to be dealt with through social legislations, but there are other problems pertaining to health, social education, vocational training, increased participation in social and cultural life, provision of shelter, and assistance to the handicapped or maladjusted call for programmes at the community level. As women have to fulfil heavy domestic and economic responsibilities, adequate attention has to be paid to the need for relaxation and recreation both in the homes as well as in the community.

4.1 Women and Family

Women play a critical role in the family which is the basic unit of society. Family is a strong force for social cohesion and integration and as such should be strengthened. The inadequate support to women and insufficient protection to their respective families affect society as a whole and undermines efforts to achieve gender equality. In different cultural, political and social systems, various forms of family exist and the rights, capabilities and responsibilities of family members must be respected.

Women's social and economic contributions to the welfare of the family and the social significance of maternity and paternity continue to be inadequately addressed. Motherhood and fatherhood and the role of parents and legal guardians in the family and in the upbringing of children and the importance of all family members in the family's well-being is also acknowledged and must not be a basis for discrimination. Women also continue to bear a disproportionate share of the household responsibilities and the care of children, the sick and the elderly. In order to achieve full partnership, both in public and private spheres, both women and men must be enabled to reconcile and share equal work and family responsibilities.

4.2 Women and Socio-economic Development

The extent of empowerment of women in the national hierarchy is determined largely by three factors: their economic, social and political identity. These factors are deeply intertwined and interlinked with many cross-cutting linkages. However, if efforts in even one dimension remain absent or weak, outcomes generated by the other components are adversely affected. Women can be truly empowered only when all the three factors are simultaneously addressed and made compatible with each other. In other words, for holistic empowerment of women to happen, economic, social and political aspects impacting women's life must converge effectively.

It is a well-acknowledged fact that the thrust on social and human development is an important plank of next generation policy reforms. The efforts are being complemented by a steep jump in budgetary outlays for social sectors, along with dedicated initiatives for removing poverty and increasing employment. Participation of women in productive activities reduces poverty, enhances economic growth and hence benefits society at large.

Women's lack of economic empowerment not only impedes growth and poverty reduction, but also has a host of other negative impacts including less favourable education and health outcomes for children. Thus, it is extremely important to ensure that women are economically empowered.

Women's contribution to the economy remains significantly invisible in national accounts. Although a certain degree of statistical invisibility of women in the economy is a global phenomenon, it is particularly predominant in India and other

South Asian nations due to their orthodox socio-cultural milieu. The United Nations Statistical Division has been active in extending the production boundary of the Systems of National Accounts (SNA), 1993 and this has led to the inclusion of the unpaid work of women in the care economy in the national accounting system as satellite accounts. This extended production boundary of SNA, 1993, provides a better understanding of women's contribution to the economy.

4.3 Women and the Environment

With privatisation, liberalisation and globalisation of the Indian economy, environment and forest sectors are also undergoing signs of change. Also, with the looming dangers of global warming and climate change, environment has emerged as a matter of great concern both at the national and international level. Environment and forests sectors are increasingly figuring as areas of interests in the bilateral, plurilateral and multilateral free trade agreements. India being a founder member of the World Trade Organization (WTO) is governed by its basic binding principles and has been actively participating in such trade negotiations. The Doha Round of trade negotiations launched in November 2001 introduced negotiations in environmental goods and services. As a result, both the environmental goods and environmental services have emerged as areas of significance for India.

In recognition of the link between gender equality, poverty eradication, sustainable development and environmental protection, governments in many countries have included income-generating activities for women, training in natural resource management and environmental protection in their development strategies. Projects have been launched to preserve and utilize women's traditional ecological knowledge, in the management of natural resources, and preservation of bio-diversity.

There is still a lack of public awareness about environmental risks faced by women and of the benefits of gender equality for promoting environmental protection. Women's limited access to technical skills, resources and information in developing countries have impeded women's effective participation in decision-making regarding the sustainable environment.

There are important gender perspectives in all aspects of climate change. Adaptation efforts must systematically and effectively address gender-specific impacts of climate change in the areas of energy, water, food security, agriculture and fisheries, biodiversity and ecosystem services, health, industry, human settlements, disaster management, and security. Gender inequalities in access to resources, including credit, extension services, information and technology, must be taken into account in developing mitigation activities.

4.3.1 Women and Natural Resources: The linkage between women, natural resources and the domestic economies of poor rural households in India are fairly clear and they can be categorized into the following three patterns.

1. Natural resources are central to the livelihoods in India. Poor households are dependent on free biomass goods and common property resources than better off households.
2. Women are the primary gatherers and managers of biomass goods in poor rural households. Women perform key roles not only in the gathering but also in the processing, storing, utilization and marketing of free biomass goods.
3. Women's roles and responsibilities are pivotal not only in the management of natural resources but also in the management of domestic economy.

Thus, natural resources provide both subsistence needs and cash incomes, particularly to poor rural households.

4.3.2 Effects of Degradation of Natural Resources on Women: In fragile ecological regions, the gradual degradation of natural resources has depleted the social resources of people such as nutrition, health (particularly of women and children), education, housing etc. With the migration of men to urban areas and increase in the responsibility and workload of women, the girl child of the family becomes victim of degradation. She has to discontinue her education in order to take care of her younger siblings and becomes their foster mother at a very young age. These girl children also attend to all domestic chores and feed the animals while the mother is miles away in the jungles to collect fuel wood and forest produces. In many rural and tribal communities, particularly among the resource poor, the following common social features/phenomena are observed:

1. Drop-out of girl from formal schools.
2. Early child marriage.
3. Early and frequent child births.
4. Malnutrition and poor health.
5. Maternal mortality.
6. Infant morbidity and mortality.
7. Large family size.
8. Poor sanitation.
9. Poverty and debts.

This social phenomenon is a clear picture of vulnerability of women to poverty. The root cause of these problems is poverty caused due to the degradation of soil, water resources and the scarcity of biomass resources to meet daily needs. In addition to this, ignorance of people also plays an important role in deteriorating the social conditions of the people leading to poor quality of life. The parents in resource poor families would like to shrug away with the responsibility of daughters by getting them married at a very young age with minimum expenses. However, they are ignorant of the fact that early child marriage would not only spoil the future of their daughter but also becomes a fragile basis for future generations.

Environmental concerns also warrant gender mainstreaming. Providing alternative sources of fuel for women especially in rural areas reduces both her drudgery with collection of firewood and exposure to pollutants. Thus, switching from fossil fuel to non-conventional fuel based systems such as green fuels (bio-mass), solar power, hydro power etc. should be stressed.

Disaster management policy should become gender

sensitive as experience has shown that women are most affected by disasters whether manmade or natural. The tendency for trafficking, sale of women and children is quite common in these extenuating circumstances. The emergency response systems in the event of such disasters should have well thought out gender relief measures to cater to afflicted women and children without any delay.

4.4 Barriers to Women's Empowerment

The barriers to women's empowerment are manifested in various ways. Deep-rooted ideologies of gender bias and discrimination like the confinement of women to the private domestic realm, restrictions on their mobility, poor access to health services, nutrition, education and employment, and exclusion from the public and political sphere continue to daunt women across the country. Other parameters that reflect the status and position of women in society are work participation rates, sex ratio in the age group of 0-6 years and gender based violence which remain heavily skewed against women. New challenges such as increased intra-country migration, changing labour markets that require new skill sets and rapidly changing technologies have also emerged.

The access of women to key social services such as health and education is a critical determinant of the status of women and their ability to participate in making society a better place. While the overall picture is one of progress in many dimensions, large gaps still remain.

Hence, the key elements for gender equity to be addressed can be clubbed under the following:

1. Economic empowerment.
2. Social and physical infrastructure.
3. Enabling legislations.
4. Women's participation in governance.
5. Inclusiveness of all categories of vulnerable women.
6. Engendering national policies/programmes.
7. Mainstreaming gender through gender budgeting.

Strong national machineries for the advancement of women and promotion of gender equality require political commitment at the highest level. Reforms to meet the challenges of the changing world are essential to ensure women's equal access to institutions and organizations. Institutional and conceptual changes are a strategic and important aspect of creating an enabling environment for the implementation of policies and programmes for the advancement of women.

Programme support to enhance women's opportunities, potentials and activities need to have a dual focus: on the one hand, programmes aimed at meeting the basic as well as the specific needs of women for capacity building, organizational development and empowerment; and on the other, gender mainstreaming in all programme formulation and implementation activities. It is particularly important to expand into new areas of programming to advance gender equality in response to current challenges.

4.5 Globalization and Women

4.5.1 Adverse Effects of Globalization on Women: With the growing globalization and liberalization of the economy as well as increased privatization of services, women as a whole have been left behind and not been able to partake of the fruits of success. Mainstreaming of women into the new and emerging areas of growth is imperative. This will require training and skill upgradation in emerging trades, encouraging more women to take up vocational training and employment in the boom sectors. This will also require women to migrate to cities and metros for work. Provision of safe housing and other gender friendly facilities at work will need to be provided.

Another facet of globalization is related to the fact that many persons, especially women, will be severely affected with the advent of setting up of industrial parks, national highways, special economic zones (SEZs) etc. as huge tracts of farm land are likely to be acquired for this purpose. This would require massive resettlement of the displaced persons and their families. It is, therefore, essential that a viable resettlement policy and strategy is formulated and put in place immediately which clearly reflects the needs of women impacted by globalization/displacement.

With the removal of all quantitative restrictions on the import of various products, the self-employed women's groups, especially in the informal sector, have started facing competition from the low-priced imported consumer goods which are invading the Indian market. Although this has the imminent danger of displacing a large number of employed/self-employed women, but at the same time, the process of globalization has also opened up opportunities for women entrepreneurs for exporting their products to the markets all over the world. Globalization has thus opened up new challenges for the realization of the goal of women's empowerment. Hence, strategies should be designed to enhance the capacity of women and empower them to cope with the negative economic and social impacts of the globalization process.

Several studies have indicated that adverse consequences of globalisation are disproportionately borne by women. Increased mechanization leading to displacement of female unskilled workers, increased migration of male workers in traditionally women-dominated areas, increase in female-headed household due to migration of males are some of the trends established in various studies.

Globalization has presented new challenges for the realization of the goal of women's equality, the gender impact of which has not been systematically evaluated fully. However, it is evident that there is a need for re-framing policies for access to employment and equality of employment. Benefits of the growing global economy have been unevenly distributed leading to wider economic disparities, the feminization of poverty, increased gender inequality through deteriorating working conditions and unsafe working environment especially in the informal economy and rural areas. Strategies need to be designed to enhance the capacity of women and empower them to meet the negative social and economic impacts, which may flow from the globalization process.

With upgradation of skills, opportunities for employment of women exist in several areas such as health services, food processing and crafts. Key areas of concern include women in small subsistence farming households, women workers in garment and textiles who will face increased competition after the phasing out of the Multi Fibre Agreement in 2005, and women displaced by new technologies in sectors such as construction, which have traditionally absorbed large numbers of women.

With the onset of trade liberalisation, women in India today are linked to the global economy to a very significant extent, as producers, entrepreneurs, service providers, consumers and citizens. There is a need to identify capacity constraints and entry barriers that prevent women from securing gains from trade. Trade-related awareness and capacity building of the women stakeholders need to be prioritised.

The globalization process has, in some countries, resulted in policy shifts in favour of more open trade and financial flows, privatization of state-owned enterprises and in many cases lower public spending particularly on social services. This change has transformed patterns of production and accelerated technological advances in information and communication and affected the lives of women, both as workers and consumers. In a large number of countries, particularly in developing and least developed countries, these changes have also adversely impacted on the lives of women and have increased inequality. The gender impact of these changes has not been systematically evaluated. Globalization has also affected cultural values, lifestyles and forms of communication.

In countries with economies in transition, women are bearing most of the hardships induced by the economic restructuring and being the first to lose jobs in times of recession. They are being squeezed out from fast growth sectors. Loss of childcare facilities due to elimination or privatization of state work places, increased need for older care without the corresponding facilities, continuing inequality of access to training for finding re-employment and to productive assets for entering or expanding businesses are current challenges facing women in these countries.

4.5.2 Opportunities Offered by Globalization: Science and technology, as fundamental components of development, are transforming patterns of production, contributing to the creation of jobs and new job classifications, and ways of working, and contributing to the establishment of a knowledge-based society. Technological change can bring new opportunities for all women in all fields if they have equal access, and adequate training. Women should also be actively involved in the definition, design, development, implementation and gender impact evaluation of policies related to these changes. Many women world-wide are yet to effectively use these new communications technologies for networking, advocacy, exchange of information business, education, media consultation and e-commerce initiatives. For instance, millions of the world's poorest women and men still do not have access to and benefits from science and technology and are currently excluded from this new field and the opportunities it presents.

The patterns of migratory flows of labour are changing. Women and girls are increasingly involved in internal, regional and international labour migration to pursue many occupations mainly in farm labour, domestic work and some forms of entertainment work. While this situation increases their earning opportunities and self-reliance, it also exposes them—particularly the poor, uneducated, unskilled and/or undocumented migrants—to inadequate working conditions, increased health risk, the risk of trafficking, economic and sexual exploitation, racism, racial discrimination and xenophobia, and other forms of abuse.

Further, globalization has dramatically changed the conditions under which the work for gender equality must be carried out, especially in high growth countries like India. While globalization has generated opportunities for local producers and entrepreneurs to reach international markets, it has at times intensified existing inequalities and insecurities for many poor women. Since the gains of globalization are often concentrated in the hands of those with higher education—those who own resources and have access to capital—poor women are usually the least able to seize the long-term opportunities offered.

This disadvantage has been exacerbated as in most of the countries, policies reflect a commitment to global norms of markets and social policy is increasingly determined by market dynamics. Market-friendly policies generate high growth rates that fail to translate into improved standards of health, education and human security. Feminist scholars have highlighted the gendered impact of such policies, many of which increase women's job vulnerability, unpaid work burden, while reducing state level resources that might be used to provide a social safety net.

Owing to dissent voiced by feminist scholars on the widespread assumption that gender inequality as a challenge can be overcome with effective and sustained advocacy as it is more about mindsets and less about policies, especially economic policies, there have been some attempts to integrate economic and social policies but gender concerns have not been accorded requisite attention. These disadvantages have led to a situation where gains in women's economic opportunities lag behind those in women's capabilities.

In a semi-industrialised country like India, the working class in destined to be one of the weaker sections of society. Moreover, society being male-dominated, female labour receives very poor recognition or value. Not that there are no statutory provisions. In fact, the Constitution of India provides equal rights and opportunities to both the genders. In addition, there are specific provisions for protection and welfare of working women in many of the labour laws. However, most of these statutes do not cover the units in small and informal sectors which are the predominant workplaces of women.

Even where they are covered by the statutes, the poor enforcement practically nullifies the provisions. Moreover, there is another tragic factor that has to be noted. The very laws which are meant for working women are paradoxically turned against their interests by unscrupulous employers. If the employers find it difficult to bypass these provisions, they get rid of the women workers and thus strike at the economic base of their livelihood. All these factors need to be studied in depth while drafting policy and legal provisions for the working women in order to plug all possible loopholes.

For the reasons mentioned above, as also for the benefit of working women, their union leaders—and for all those who are interested in the welfare of women workers—knowledge of existing provisions of labour laws is very essential. Women emancipation is part of India's general developmental plans but government action can be neither effective nor adequate unless women themselves become more aware of their rights and the corresponding responsibilities. Every woman is a working woman, whether she works in the home or outside it. Many women work to earn money. Working women must know that they have some basic rights which are given by the law.

Though India has created protective legislations for women, the enactments have not been easy to implement. The very vastness of the country, the scattered nature of women workers, their lack of education and legal literacy, indifferent attitude of bureaucracy and the general status of women in society have added to vulnerability of women. This is true not only of rural unorganised women, but to an extent of the urban women workers also.

The overall picture that emerges is one of greater disadvantage for women workers in general and those belonging to rural as well as scheduled castes (SCs)/scheduled tribes (STs) in particular. Apart from such inherited disadvantages as lower social position, a number of other factors also contribute to such a picture. These are their limited asset position, access to resources, and low level of education and skill. Education, and consequently some ability to acquire formal skills, could be a moderating force but this aspect presents a dismal picture. The overall situation of women workers calls for interventions of a promotional nature from different entry points but with a strong emphasis on education.

5

Constitutional and Legal Safeguards for Women

Women constitute roughly half of India's population. The importance of women is recognised by the Constitution of India which not only accords equality to women but also empowers the State to adopt measures for positive discrimination in their favour.

5.1 Constitutional Provisions for Women

The Constitution of India adopted on November 26, 1949, became operative on January 26, 1950. It provides for two layers of Government, one at the Central level, and the other at the level of the States.

The Constitution of India recognises the right of women to employment and includes a number of Articles to give direction to the state policy. Article 14 lays down the equality before law of all citizens of the country, and Article 15 prohibits discrimination on the grounds of sex, religion, race etc. Articles 16(1) and (2) emphasise equal opportunities for all in the matter of employment and prohibits discrimination in employment.

Article 15(3) of the Constitution empowers the state to make special provisions for women and children within the framework of the fundamental rights. Articles 39 and 42 specially refer to women and children. They direct the State to secure health and strength of all workers, men, women and children and not to abuse children for economic gains. Humane and just conditions of work and maternity benefit are assured to women by Article 42.

Thus, labour legislation for women in India is rooted in the Indian constitution and is guided by ILO conventions. The objective of these enactments is to protect women from exploitation.

There are Articles in the Constitution which reiterate commitment of the nation towards the socio- economic development of women and upholding their political rights and participation in decision-making (Table 5.1).

Table 5.1: Provisions in the Constitution of India for Socio-economic Development of Women

Article	Brief Description
Article 14	Men and women to have equal rights and opportunities in the political, economic and social spheres.
Article 15(1)	Prohibits discrimination against any citizen on the grounds of religion, race, caste, sex etc.
Article 15(3)	Special provision enabling the State to make affirmative discriminations in favour of women.
Article 16	Equality of opportunities in matter of public appointments for all citizens.
Article 39(a)	State shall direct its policy towards securing all citizens men and women, equally, the right to means of livelihood.
Article 39(d)	Equal pay for equal work for both men and women.
Article 42	State to make provision for ensuring just and humane conditions of work and maternity relief.
Article 51 (A)(e)	To renounce the practices derogatory to the dignity of women.

5.2 Legislations for Protection and Advancement of Women

Drawing the strength from the constitutional commitments, the Government of India has been engaged in the continuous endeavour of concretely translating all the rights, commitments and safeguards incorporated in the Indian Constitution for women from *de jure* to *de facto* status.

5.2.1 Objectives of Women-specific Legislations: The objectives of various legislations enacted include the following:

1. Creating an environment through positive economic and social policies for full development of women to enable them to realize their full potential.
2. Enjoyment of all human rights and fundamental freedom by women on equal basis with men in all spheres—political, economic, social, cultural and civil.
3. Equal access to participation and decision-making of women in social, political and economic life of the nation.
4. Equal access to women for health care, quality education at all levels, career and vocational guidance, employment, remuneration, occupational health and safety, social security and public office.
5. Strengthening legal systems aimed at elimination of all forms of discrimination against women.
6. Changing societal attitudes and community practices by active participation and involvement of both men and women.
7. Mainstreaming a gender perspective in the development process.
8. Elimination of discrimination and all forms of violence against women and the girl child.
9. Building and strengthening partnerships with civil society, particularly women's organizations.

5.3 Laws Related to Dowry, Marriage and Divorce

These are the following:

5.3.1 Christian Marriage Act, 1872: This Act governs the Christian law of marriage in India. Marriage, as is seen in Christian tradition, is not merely a civil contract nor is it purely a religious contract. It is seen as a contract according to the law of nature, antecedent to civil institutions and by itself an institution. A marriage among Christians is traditionally understood as the voluntary union for life of one man and one woman to the exclusion of all others, and Indian law follows suit, so that India does not allow for the possibility of same-sex marriage as it has been celebrated by some churches in other countries in recent years.

5.3.2 Special Marriage Act, 1954: The main reason behind passing this Act was to provide a special form of marriage for the people of India and all Indian nationals in foreign countries, irrespective of the religion or faith followed by either party. The enactment has the following 3 major objectives:

1. To provide a special form of marriage in certain cases.
2. To provide for registration of certain marriages.
3. To provide for divorce.

5.3.3 Hindu Marriage Act, 1955: Hindu Marriage Act of 1955 amended in 1976 provides the right for girls to repudiate a child marriage before attaining maturity whether the marriage has been consummated or not.

5.3.4 Dowry Prohibition Act, 1961: An amendment brought in 1984 to the Dowry Prohibition Act of 1961 made women's subjection to cruelty a cognizable offence. The second amendment brought in 1986 makes the husband or in-laws punishable, if a woman commits suicide within 7 years of her marriage and it has been proved that she has been subjected to cruelty. Also a new criminal offence of *dowry death* has been incorporated in the Indian Penal Code.

5.3.5 Foreign Marriage Act, 1969: This is an Act to make provision relating to marriages of citizens of India outside India.

5.3.6 Marriage (Amendment) Act, 2001: It amended the Hindu Marriage Act, Special Marriage Act, Parsi Marriage and Divorce Act, and the Code of Criminal Procedure providing for speedy disposal of applications for maintenance; the ceiling limit for claiming maintenance has been deleted and a wide discretion has been given to the magistrate to award appropriate maintenance.

5.3.7 Prohibition of Child Marriage Act, 2006: Child

Marriage Restraint Act of 1976 raised the age for marriage of a girl to 18 years from 15 years and that of a boy to 21 years and made offences under this Act cognizable. Child marriages in India have continued unabated despite the enactment of laws for its restraint and prohibition. Early marriages have adverse consequences on women's growth, health, livelihood options and negotiating power within marriages. In addition, criminal provisions on kidnapping and abduction can also be used to penalize those involved in child marriages. The status of a child marriage, i.e. whether it is void or voidable, is governed by marriage laws that are applicable to different religious communities.

5.4 Laws Related to Right to Property

These are as follows:

5.4.1 Muslim Personal Law (Shariat) Application Act, 1937: This is an Act to make provision for the application of the Muslim Personal Law (Shariat) to Muslims.

5.4.2 Hindu Succession Act, 1956: This Act is a law that was passed by the Parliament of India in 1956 to amend and codify the law relating to intestate or unwilled succession, among Hindus. The Act lays down a uniform and comprehensive system of inheritance and applies to persons governed by both the Mitākṣarā and Dāyabhāga schools. It is hailed for its consolidation of Hindu laws on succession into one Act. The Hindu woman's limited estate is abolished by the Act. Any property possessed by a Hindu female is to be held by her absolute property and she is given full power to deal with it and dispose it of by will as she likes. The Act was amended in 2005 by the Hindu Succession (Amendment) Act, 2005.

5.5 Laws Related to Protection of and Crimes against Women

These are the following:

5.5.1 Crimes Identified under Indian Penal Code (IPC):

1. Rape (Section 376 IPC).
2. Kidnapping and abduction for different purposes (Section

363-373 IPC).

3. Homicide for Dowry, Dowry Deaths or their attempts (Section 302/304-B of IPC).
4. Torture, both mental and physical (Section 498-A of IPC).
5. Molestation (Section 354 of IPC).
6. Sexual harassment (Section 509 of IPC) (referred to in the past as Eve teasing).
7. Importation of girls (up to 21 years of age) (Section 366-B of IPC).

5.5.2 Crimes Identified under the Special Laws

A. Immoral Traffic (Prevention) Act, 1956: As amended and renamed in 1986, the Act makes the sexual exploitation of male or female, a cognizable offence. It is being amended to decriminalize the prostitutes and make the laws more stringent against traffickers.

B. Medical Termination Pregnancy Act, 1971: It legalises abortion by qualified professional on humanitarian or medical grounds. The maximum punishment may go up to life imprisonment. The Act has further been amended specifying the place and persons authorized to perform abortion and provide for penal actions against the unauthorized persons performing abortions.

C. Indecent Representation of Women (Prohibition) Act, 1986: The Act aims to protect the dignity of women and prevent violence against them as well as their exploitation.

D. Commission of Sati (Prevention) Act, 1987: The aim of the Act is to protect the dignity of women and prevent violence against them as well as their exploitation.

E. Pre-Natal Diagnostic Techniques (Regulation and Prevention of Misuse) Act, 1994: The sex ratio in India has been unfavourable to girls. Legal action to stop female foeticide dates back to the enactment of this Act which was an attempt to reduce the imbalance in sex ratio. Keeping in view the emerging technologies, the Act was amended in 2002 to tighten enforcement.

F. Pre-conception and Pre-natal Diagnostic Techniques (Prohibition of Sex Selection) Act, 2003: This Act has broadened the existing ban on sex determination to prompt the use of preconception and pre-implementation gene diagnosis and other technologies for sex selection. Use of ultrasound machines has been brought within the purview of this Act. Other new provisions include maintenance of written records of procedures carried out (not previously required) by doctors, and the vesting in state, district and sub district level authorities of powers equivalent to civil courts to ensure compliance with the law and to follow up reports on violation and misconduct.

Other relevant legislative enactments include amendment to the Medical Termination of Pregnancy Act 1971, (amended in 2002) which includes specific punishments for conduct of illegal abortions by unqualified persons and at places not approved by the concerned authority. Moreover, the authority has been decentralised to district health officers.

G. Protection of Women from Domestic Violence Act (PWDVA), 2006: Domestic violence against women though pervasive is a largely invisible crime and goes unrecognized, especially since domestic violence is considered as a family matter having an unspoken sanction in patriarchal society. There is very little data on the extent of domestic violence.

Domestic violence is a term that is difficult to define as the violence occurs against women in intimate relationships. A victim of domestic violence tends to shield the perpetrator of violence in keeping with her socio cultural psyche and value system.

In order to address the phenomenon of domestic violence, which is widely prevalent but remains largely invisible in the public domain, PWDVA, 2006 was enacted by the Parliament. The Act envisages that the protection officer would assist the victim of domestic violence to be secure from violence and help her to access shelter homes, healthcare and legal advice. Harassment relating to dowry has also been covered under this Act.

H. Sexual Harassment of Women at Workplace (Prevention, Prohibition and Redressal) Act, 2013:

(a) Background: As enshrined in the Preamble to the Constitution of India, "equality of status and opportunity" must be secured for all its citizens; equality of every person under the law is guaranteed by Article 14 of the Constitution.

A safe workplace is therefore a woman's legal right. Indeed, the Constitutional doctrine of equality and personal liberty is contained in Articles 14, 15 and 21 of the Indian Constitution. These articles ensure a person's right to equal protection under the law, to live a life free from discrimination on any ground and to protection of life and personal liberty. This is further reinforced by the UN Convention on the Elimination of all Forms of Discrimination against Women (CEDAW), which was adopted by the UN General Assembly in 1979 and which is ratified by India. Often described as an international bill of rights for women, it calls for the equality of women and men in terms of human rights and fundamental freedoms in the political, economic, social, cultural and civil spheres. It underlines that discrimination and attacks on women's dignity violate the principle of equality of rights.

Sexual harassment constitutes a gross violation of women's right to equality and dignity. It has its roots in patriarchy and its attendant perception that men are superior to women and that some forms of violence against women are acceptable. One of these is workplace sexual harassment, which views various forms of such harassment, as harmless and trivial. Often, it is excused as 'natural' male behaviour or 'harmless flirtation' which women enjoy. Contrary to these perceptions, it causes serious harm and is also a strong manifestation of sex discrimination at the workplace. Not only is it an infringement of the fundamental rights of a woman, under Article 19(1)(g) of the Constitution of India which says, "to practice any profession or to carry out any occupation, trade or business"; it erodes equality and puts the dignity and the physical and psychological well-being of workers at risk.

This leads to poor productivity and a negative impact on lives and livelihoods.

To further compound the matter, deep-rooted socio-cultural behavioural patterns, which create a gender hierarchy, tend to place responsibility on the victim, thereby increasing inequality in the workplace and in the society at large.

Though sexual harassment at the workplace has assumed serious proportions, women do not report the matter to the concerned authorities in most cases due to fear of reprisal from the harasser, losing one's livelihood, being stigmatized, or losing professional standing and personal reputation.

Across the globe today, workplace sexual harassment is increasingly understood as a violation of women's rights and a form of violence against women. Indeed, the social construct of male privileges in society continues to be used to justify violence against women in the private and public sphere. In essence, sexual harassment is a mirror reflecting male power over women that sustains patriarchal relations. In a society where violence against women, both subtle and direct, is borne out of the patriarchal values, women are forced to conform to traditional gender roles. These patriarchal values and attitudes of both women and men pose the greatest challenge in resolution and prevention of sexual harassment. Workplace sexual harassment, like other forms of violence, is not harmless. It involves serious health, human, economic and social costs, which manifest themselves in the overall development indices of a nation.

The Sexual Harassment of Women at Workplace (Prevention, Prohibition and Redressal) Act, 2013, was enacted to ensure safe working spaces for women and to build enabling work environments that respect women's right to equality of status and opportunity. An effective implementation of the Act will contribute to the realization of their right to gender equality, life and liberty, equality in working conditions everywhere. The sense of security at the workplace will improve women's participation in work, resulting in their economic empowerment and inclusive growth.

The full scale of the problem is not known given the difficulties in documenting the experience of those who have experienced workplace sexual harassment. However, available studies on sexual harassment show that it is certainly prevalent in India today. This is why the legislation is an important step forward within the larger architecture of women's rights, as it tackles this issue to secure the rights of women workers across the country.

While the official figures for women's work participation are low, much of the work that women do is not captured in official data accounts. It is argued that where this is to be captured, women's overall work participation would be 86.2 percent. While the official data shows that women's work participation rate is around 25.3 percent in rural areas and 14.7 percent in the urban areas, estimates indicate that there is a huge workforce of women, therefore there is a need to secure their workplace and entitlements. Given, that 93 percent of women workers are employed in the informal sector, they remain unprotected by laws. With no laws or mechanisms to protect them, proactive measures are required to make their workplaces safe.

It is well-established that ensuring safe working conditions for women leads to a positive impact on their participation in the workforce and increases their productivity, which in turn benefits the nation as a whole. Economically, empowered women are key to the nation's overall development and this can only be achieved if it is ensured that women's workspaces across all sectors and all over the country have a safe and secure environment for work.

It is important as well to ensure that the emphasis is on prevention rather than punitive action. This calls for widespread awareness on the Act among employers, managers and the workers themselves. Frequently, women workers may face sexual harassment but may not be aware that it is a breach of their rights and that there is something they can do about it.

They need to know that they can do something about it. Then there are others, who may believe that it is a personal matter that needs to be resolved by the people involved. In order to change this order of things, it is urgent that measures are taken to change mind-sets and attitudes by creating awareness about what constitutes sexual harassment and the steps that can be taken to address it.

Today, all workplaces in India are mandated by law to provide a safe and secure working environment free from sexual harassment for all women.

(b) The Genesis: In 1992, a rural level change agent, Bhanwari Devi, was engaged by the state of Rajasthan as a Sathin (friend) to work towards the prevention of the practice of child marriages. During the course of her work, she prevented the marriage of a one-year old girl in the community. Her work was met with resentment and attracted harassment from men of that community. Bhanwari Devi reported this to the local authority but no action was taken. That omission came at great cost—Bhanwari was subsequently gang raped by those very men.

The Bhanwari Devi case revealed the ever-present sexual harm to which millions of working women are exposed across the country, everywhere and everyday irrespective of their location. It also shows the extent to which that harm can escalate if nothing is done to check sexually offensive behaviour in the workplace.

Based on the facts of Bhanwari Devi's case, a public interest litigation (PIL) was filed by Vishaka and other women groups against the State of Rajasthan and Union of India before the Supreme Court of India. It proposed that sexual harassment be recognized as a violation of women's fundamental right to equality and that all workplaces, establishments and institutions be made accountable and responsible to uphold these rights.

In a landmark judgment in the case of *Vishaka vs. State of Rajasthan* (1997), the Supreme Court of India created legally binding guidelines basing it on the right to equality and dignity accorded under the Indian Constitution as well as by the UN Convention on the Elimination of All Forms of Discrimination against Women (CEDAW). It included:

- A definition of sexual harassment.
- Shifting accountability from individuals to institutions.
- Prioritizing prevention.
- Provision of an innovative redress mechanism.

The Supreme Court defined sexual harassment as any unwelcome, sexually determined physical, verbal, or non-verbal conduct. Examples included sexually suggestive remarks about women, demands for sexual favours, and sexually offensive visuals in the workplace. The definition also covered situations where a woman could be disadvantaged in her workplace as a result of threats relating to employment decisions that could negatively affect her working life.

It placed responsibility on employers to ensure that women did not face a hostile environment, and prohibited intimidation or victimization of those cooperating with an inquiry, including the affected complainant as well as witnesses.

It directed for the establishment of redressal mechanism in the form of complaints committee, which will look into the matters of sexual harassment of women at workplace. The complaints committees were mandated to be headed by a woman employee, with not less than half of its members being women and provided for the involvement of a third party person/NGO expert on the issue, to prevent any undue pressure on the complainant. The guidelines extended to all kinds of employment, from paid to voluntary, across the public and private sectors.

Vishaka established that international standards/law could serve to expand the scope of India's Constitutional guarantees and fill in the gaps wherever they exist. India's innovative history in tackling workplace sexual harassment beginning with the Vishaka Guidelines and subsequent legislation has given critical visibility to the issue. Workplaces must now own their responsibility within this context and ensure that women can work in safe and secure spaces.

(c) The Act: Having raised the bar of responsibility and accountability in the Vishaka Guidelines, the Supreme Court placed an obligation on workplaces, institutions and those in positions of responsibility, to uphold working women's fundamental right to equality and dignity at the workplace. Three key obligations were imposed on institutions to meet that standard, namely:

- Prohibition,
- Prevention, and
- Redress.

In 2013, the Government of India notified the Sexual Harassment of Women at Workplace (Prevention, Prohibition and Redressal) Act (referred to as Act hereinafter). Consistent with the Vishaka judgment, the Act aspires to ensure women's right to workplace equality, free from sexual harassment through compliance with the above mentioned three elements.

It is important to note that the Act provides a civil remedy to women and is in addition to other laws that are currently in force. Consequently, any woman who wishes to report instances of sexual harassment at the workplace has the right to take recourse of both civil and criminal proceedings.

5.6 Laws Related to Protection of Rights of Working Women

The laws which are applicable to women workers in India can be broadly divided into three categories.

5.6.1 Category I Laws: Laws of this category include laws which are exclusively meant for women, the important ones being the following:

A. Maternity Benefit Act (MBA), 1961: Performance of the biological role of child bearing necessarily involves withdrawal of a woman from the workforce for some period. During this period she not only cannot work for her living but needs extra income for her medical expenses. In order to enable the woman worker to subsist during this period and to preserve her health, the law makes a provision for maternity benefit so that the woman can play her productive and reproductive roles efficiently.

One of the earliest conventions adopted by International Labour Organization (ILO) was the Maternity Protection Convention, 1919 the purpose of which was to provide protection to women workers in certain conditions. All the member countries of ILO were directed to pass suitable legislation to extend certain benefits to women during pregnancy and after childbirth. India being one of the founder members of ILO was expected to pass such legislation without delay.

It was the Government of the State of Bombay that enacted the first maternity benefit legislation in the year 1929. The Act provided for a leave of 7 weeks and an allowance of 50 paise per day during the leave period, for any woman worker who was due for delivery. To be eligible to receive this benefit the woman should have worked in that factory or establishment for at least a period of 6 months. This legislation was regarded as very progressive. Soon, some other states followed the example of Bombay state and enacted similar laws with some minor variations.

It was in the year 1961 that the Central Government with a view to bringing some uniformity in the provisions of various maternity protection acts, passed what is known as the Maternity Benefit Act, 1961. Article 42 of the Constitution of India requires that the State should make provision, *inter alia*, for maternity relief.

MBA, 1961 applies to all factories, establishments, plantations, mines, and shops where 10 or more persons are employed. Maternity benefits are also provided under the Employees State Insurance (ESI) Act, 1948 and an insured woman is entitled to maternity benefit in the form of periodical payments in case of confinement, miscarriage or sickness arising out of pregnancy. They are also entitled to medical care under the ESI Scheme for maternity, and where medical facilities are not available they are paid a specified sum for the purpose. The provisions in the ESI Act for medical benefit are more comprehensive than those under the MBA 1961, in so far as they include medical care, and pre- and post-natal care. The factories or the establishments to which the provisions of the ESI Scheme apply are excluded from the purview of the Act of 1961.

MBA, 1961 is administered by State Governments. There are comprehensive regulatory provisions. Women employees who complete 80 days of work prior to delivery are entitled to maternity benefits.

MBA, 1961 provides for payment of cash maternity benefits for certain periods before or after confinement, grant of leave and other medical facilities. This benefit is available in case of confinement, miscarriage, sickness arising out of pregnancy and premature birth of the child. In 1995, MBA, 1961 was amended to extend the benefits to women undergoing tubectomy, medical termination of pregnancy (MTP) and for any illness arising out of MTP or tubectomy.

B. Equal Remuneration Act (ERA), 1976: ERA, 1976 provides for the prevention of discrimination on the ground of sex against women in the matter of employment and for matters connected therewith or incidental thereto. It also prohibits discrimination while recruiting men and women workers for the same or similar nature of work except where the employment of women in such work is restricted or prohibited by or under any law for the time being.

Till 1975, there was no specific legal provision mandating payment of equal wages to women even though discrimination against women in the payment of wages was widely rampant. Such discrimination was practised not only by private employers but by the instruments of the state as well. The First National Commission on Labour (1969) had found that in agriculture and small industries—the large sectors where women were employed—some State Governments had been fixing differential wages rates.

This situation continued in spite of the fact that Article 15 of the Constitution specifically prohibits discrimination against women. The provision relating to *equal pay for equal work* is not an enforceable fundamental right but is issued as a directive to the state in Part IV of the Constitution. By this, the state was obliged to secure such social and economic freedoms for the citizens which could not be guaranteed at the time when the Constitution was framed due to the then prevalent socio-economic conditions.

In 1951, ILO passed a convention called Equal Remuneration Convention (No. 100), the full title of which is "Equal Remuneration for Men and Women Workers for Work for Equal Value". With a view to honour this ILO convention and also to implement Article 39 (equal pay for equal work, for both men and women) of the Indian Constitution, the President of India promulgated an ordinance in September 1975 (i.e. in the International Women's Year) called Equal Remuneration Ordinance. After receiving the consent of the parliament it was turned into Equal Remuneration Act of 1976 according to which if a man and a woman do the same kind of work, they must get equal wages. It does not mean only work which is identical in all respects but also work which can broadly be considered to be same or similar in nature to the other work.

ERA, 1976 places duty on the employer to pay equal remuneration to men and women workers employed by him in an establishment or employment for performing same or similar nature of work. It forbids discrimination against women workers either at the time of recruitment or in any condition of service subsequent to recruitment such as promotion, training or transfer. This protection does not extend to places where the employment of women is prohibited or restricted by any other law in force.

In order to promote employment opportunities for women, ERA, 1976 provides for setting up advisory committees and appropriate authorities to hear and decide claims and complaints arising out of the Act. With the aim of providing increasing options for women including part-time employment, the advisory committees are required to inform the government of the extent to which women may be employed in specified establishments duly considering the nature and hours of work and suitability of women for that employment. The inclusion of this provision shows recognition of the need to look into the quantitative aspect of women's employment.

5.6.2 Category II Laws: This category covers those laws which are not exclusively for women but are meant for all workers, and yet contain certain sections or provisions especially for women. These sex-neutral laws include the following:

A. Factories Act, 1948: This Act is the principal legislation for regulating various aspects relating to safety, health and welfare of workers employed in factories. It aims at protecting workers employed in factories from industrial and occupational hazards. The Act prescribes a 48 hour week for adult workers and forbids employment of children under 14 years of age in any factory. Minimum standards of lighting, ventilation, safety and welfare services which employers must provide in their factories have also been laid down.

The Act is important as it contains certain provisions regarding the nature of work to be given to women workers, hours of work for them, etc. It also makes arrangements for certain welfare amenities.

B. Plantation Labour Act, 1951: Plantation is an important industry as far as employment of women is concerned.

The Act lays down conditions for the registration of plantations by the owners and also has provision regarding health, safety and welfare of the workers. A peculiar feature of employment in plantations is that the entire family of a worker is employed. The worker usually lives on the site and he, his wife, and adolescent children all work in the plantations in different capacities. Hence the unit of employment is the family, not the individual. Women mainly work as pluckers in tea and coffee plantations.

The Act defines the term *family* as follows: The worker, his or her spouse, legitimate or adopted children depending on him who have not completed 18 years of age, and where the worker is a male, his parents dependent on him.

Every plantation has to be registered and it is mandatory on the owner to provide certain health facilities and housing for all workers. The following are the provisions for health.

1. Cool drinking water must be provided near the sites where the workers are working.
2. Separate latrines and urinals must be provided for male and female workers.
3. Medical facilities must be made available for the worker and his family. In case the employer does not provide these, the Chief Inspector of Plantations should arrange to provide them and make the employer pay the cost.

The following are the provisions for welfare of workers.

Canteen facility must be provided in every plantation which employs 150 or more workers.

Wherever 50 or more women (including women workers employed by contractors) are employed or were employed on any day in the previous 12 months, or where the number of children under 6 years of women employed in the plantation exceeds 20, a fully equipped crèche must be provided by the owner. Even if the number of women employees is less than 50, the State Governments may order that a separate room should be provided for their children.

Every plantation must provide certain recreational facilities for the workers and their families. The details of the requirement would be laid down by the State Government concerned.

When children between 6 and 10 years on any plantation exceed 25, the owner must provide educational facilities for them. The details of the requirement should be specified by the State Government concerned.

Housing has to be provided for every worker and his family residing in the plantation, and for every worker and his family residing outside the plantation but wanting to stay on the plantation, provided such worker has been working in the plantation for at least 6 months.

In case the house provided by the management collapses resulting in an injury to the worker or his family, adequate compensation must be paid by the management.

The Act also lays down that women and children must not be employed for night work. They should work only between 6 a.m. and 7 p.m.

A fitness certificate must be obtained from a doctor by all children and adolescents who desire to work on the plantation.

Women working in plantations are also covered by the Maternity Benefit Act of 1961. Hence they are also eligible to get full pay leave for 6 weeks together with the medical bonus.

As in all the other laws, in this Act also, there is a provision for inspectors who are to visit the plantation estates and see that the Act is being implemented. Penalties are also provided for the violation of the provisions.

C. Mines Act, 1952: It provides for safety, health and welfare of workers employed in mines. Provisions of the Act and the rules and regulations framed under it are enforced by the Ministry of Labour through the Directorate General of Mines Safety. The main functions of the Directorate General are: inspection of mines, investigation of all fatal accidents, approval of mines/safety equipment, exemptions and relaxations in respect of various mining operations.

Although gender-neutral, the Act has some provisions especially for women.

Mines are of two types, surface and underground. Every underground mine also has some aspects of the work which is carried out on the surface. When the ore is taken out from the deep mines it is to be loaded on trucks or wagons etc. Women are employed in this loading operation. Women also do the same type of work in open quarries. Sometimes they are employed for breaking stones.

In the Act, apart from the usual sections regarding the

licensing of mines, inspection, penalties etc., the following provisions are especially meant for women.

1. Separate latrines and urinals are to be provided for men and women working in mines. The number of latrines and urinals is fixed by the State Government according to the size of the employment at that mine.
2. No woman or child is to work below ground. They must be given work only on the surface.
3. No night work is allowed for women. They have to work only between 6 a.m. and 7 p.m. In special cases or for some special type of work, the State Government may relax the time limit up to 10 p.m. at night and 5 a.m. in the morning.

Under the Act, the Central Government is authorised to make rules requiring the mines to maintain crèches if a certain number of women workers are employed in the preceding 12 months. Thus, the Mines Crèche Rules, 1966 makes it obligatory for the owner, agent or manager of every mine, wherein women are employed or were employed on any day of the preceding 12 months, to provide a crèche at his colliery. Each crèche is required to have a trained nurse and the prescribed set of equipment. Supply of food to the children attending crèche is also obligatory on the part of the management. No limit of the number of women employees is stated. However, the State Government may grant exemption to some employers if it is found that the number of women of children is very small, or the place where the mine is situated is not at all suitable.

Four types of crèches have been specified as A, B, C and D according to the size of the room or rooms to be provided and the equipment and facilities. Details of latrines, bathrooms, furniture, medicines, first aid, toys, uniforms for the staff etc., have been given in the schedule. Cool water, milk and medicines are to be provided for children. There has to be a medical examination of the child every month, and of the nursing mothers after every 2 months. Records of medical examination must be kept for which formats are specified. Crèche must be supervised by a competent and trained person and it is to remain open day and night.

As in any other industry, women working in mines are also covered by the Maternity Benefit Act of 1961 and are eligible to get the maternity benefits.

5.6.3. Category III Laws: This category consists of laws which are neither meant exclusively for women nor contain any special provisions for women, yet they are of great significance to women workers in the unorganised sector. These are the following:

A. Minimum Wages Act, 1948: This Act empowers the Government to fix minimum wages for employees working in specified employments. Payment of overtime in scheduled employments is also governed by this Act.

Based on the recommendations of the Central Advisory Board, the Central Government recommends a National Minimum Wage and all states are requested to ensure fixation of wages in all the scheduled employments at a rate not below the recommended national minimum wage.

The Act is applicable to the workers engaged in the scheduled employments and provides for fixing minimum rates of wages in certain employments. It is applicable both to agricultural, non-agricultural and to rural as well as urban workers. The Government may, however, increase the scope of this Act by adding schedules. Units employing even one worker are covered by the Act. Thus, the Act covers wage worker, home worker but not the self-employed. Supreme Court in the case of Bandhua Mukti Morcha (1984) held that even a piece-rated worker is entitled for minimum wages.

Under the Act, the appropriate government fixes the minimum rates of wages payable to employees in a specified employment and reviews the rates at such intervals as it may think fit, such intervals not exceeding 5 years. The Government also fixes a minimum rate of wages for time-rated work, a minimum rate of wages for piece work, a minimum rate of remuneration to apply in the case of employees on piece-work for the purpose of securing to such employees a minimum rate of wages on a time work basis, a minimum rate (whether a time rate or a piece rate) to apply in substitution for the minimum rate which would otherwise be applicable, in respect of overtime work done by employees.

Different minimum rates of wages may be fixed for: (a) different scheduled employments, (b) different classes of work in the same scheduled employment, (c) adults, adolescents, children and apprentices, and (d) different localities. Similarly, minimum rates of wages may be fixed by the hour, day, month, or by such other larger wage period as may be prescribed. Any minimum rate of wages fixed or revised by the Government in respect of the scheduled employments may consist of a basic rate of wages and cost of living allowance or a basic rate of wages with or without the cost of living allowance, and the cash value of the concessions in respect of supplies of essential commodities at concessional rates, or, an all-inclusive rate allowing for the basic rate, the cost of living allowance and the cash value of the concessions.

Minimum wages are generally payable in cash unless authorised by the Government considering the prevailing custom or practice. Further, the Government may: (a) fix the number of hours of work which shall constitute a normal working day, inclusive of one or more specified intervals, (b) provide for a day of rest in every period of 7 days which shall be allowed to all employees or to any specified class of employees and for the payment of remuneration in respect of such days of rest, and (c) provide for payment for work on a day of rest at a rate not less than the overtime rate. Under the Rules, Sunday is the weekly day of rest ordinarily. For an adult 9 hours and for a child 4½ hours constitute a normal working day. Overtime is payable at 1½ times the wage in agriculture and double the rate in other cases of scheduled employment.

The subject of national minimum wages has been considered by several bodies in the past. The National

Commission on Labour (1969) was of the view that such a wage in the sense of uniform minimum monetary remuneration for the country as a whole is neither feasible nor desirable.

B. Contract Labour (Regulation and Abolition) Act, 1970: It provides for regulation of employment of contract labour in certain establishments and for its abolition in certain circumstances. It fixes responsibility on the principal employer for payment of wages in case of defaults.

This Act is applicable to every establishment in which 20 or more workmen are employed or were employed on any day of the preceding 12 months as contract labour and to every contractor who employs or who employed 20 or more workmen on any day preceding 12 months. However, the appropriate government may, after giving not less than 2 months notice and by notification in the Official Gazette, apply the provisions of this Act to any establishment or contractor employing less than 20 workmen.

This Act does not apply to establishments in which work of only an intermittent or casual nature is performed. Workman means any person employed in or in connection with the work of any establishment to do any skilled, semi-skilled or unskilled manual, supervisory, technical or clerical work for hire or reward, whether the terms of employment be express or implied. It does not include any person employed mainly in a managerial or administrative capacity; or a person employed in a supervisory capacity drawing wages exceeding ₹ 500 per month or an out-worker (home worker).

Under the Act, the appropriate government may prohibit employment of contract labour in any process, operation or other work in any establishment, having regard to the conditions of work and benefits provided for the contract labour in that establishment and other relevant factors, such as whether nature of work is incidental or necessary to the main operation, whether it is of perennial nature, that is to say, it has sufficient duration, whether it is done ordinarily through regular workmen in that/other establishment(s), and whether it is sufficient to employ considerable number of whole time workmen.

The Act also provides for licence to be taken subject to such conditions including, in particular, as to hours of work, fixation of wages and other essential amenities in respect of contract labour. The Act also contains provisions regarding welfare and health of contract labour, e.g. canteens, rest rooms, other facilities such as drinking water, urinals and, first aid facilities. For security of payment of wages, the Act provides for its payment by the contractor, and in case of failure by the principal employer.

C. Beedi and Cigar Workers (Conditions of Employment) Act, 1966: The Act is applicable to the workers engaged in beedi and cigar establishments. It regulates the conditions of their work. It applies to wage workers and home workers but not to self-employed workers/persons in private dwellings/houses.

The Act provides for cleanliness of industrial premises free from effluvia arising from any drain, privy or other nuisance. It seeks to maintain cleanliness including white washing, colour washing, varnishing, or painting. In order to prevent injury to the health of the workers, the industrial premise has to maintain proper lighting, ventilation and temperature. To prevent overcrowding, the Act prescribes at least four and a quarter cubic metres of space for every person in the workroom. It also provides for sufficient supply of wholesome drinking water, sufficient latrine and urinal accommodation, adequate washing facilities, crèches, adequate first aid facilities and canteens. It also provides for working hours in any one day and in any week, overtime, interval for rest, spread over in any day, weekly holidays, substituted holiday etc. There is prohibition of employment of children altogether and prohibition of employment of women during hours except between 6 a.m. and 7 p.m. It also contains provisions regarding annual leave with wages and wages during the leave period.

The Act applies to the entire country except the state of

Jammu & Kashmir. Any person who wants to start this industry in his place or any other place, must first obtain a license from the government. The license is granted only if the authorities are satisfied that the place is suitable and that the employer would be able to take care of the welfare of the workers employed.

This Act is of special significance for women in the unorganised sector as a large number of women work in this industry. In fact, there are more women than men. The Act also contains some special provisions for women workers.

Three provisions in the Act are important as far as women workers are concerned. In the first place, while defining the word *employer*, the Act includes *home workers,* i.e. those workers whom the contractor supplies raw material which they process in their homes. Due to the inclusion of *home workers* in the definition, those workers who roll beedis at home are also entitled to same benefits which a worker in the factory gets. Hence, this provision in the Act is of importance to women.

The second important provision is for a crèche for the infants and babies of women workers. The Act stipulates that every industrial premises, where more than 60 female employees are ordinarily employed, should maintain a crèche which is clean and well-ventilated and which is under the charge of a trained woman.

The third provision is a restriction on night work. No woman or child is to be asked to work before 6 a.m. or after 7 p.m. Of course, this provision applies only to those women workers who work in a factory or premises of the employer. If they are home workers, their working at night is not restricted.

In addition to this Act, there is a Beedi Workers Welfare Act also which prescribes provision for hospital etc. for beedi workers and their families.

D. Inter-State Migrant Workmen (Regulation of Employment and Conditions of Service) Act, 1979: The Act is applicable to every establishment in which 5 or more inter-state migrant workmen are employed and to every contractor who employs 5 or more inter-state migrant workmen. The establishments engaging less than 5 inter-state migrant workmen are not covered under this Act. For the purposes of this Act, *workman* means any person employed in or in connection with the work of any establishment to do any skilled, semi-skilled or unskilled, manual, supervisory, technical or clerical work for hire or reward, but does not include any person who is employed mainly in a managerial or administration capacity; or who, being employed in a supervisory capacity, draws wages exceeding ₹ 500 per month.

The Act provides that the wage rates, holidays, hours of work and other conditions of service of an inter-state migrant workman shall be the same as those applicable to such other workman performing the same or similar kind of work and cannot be less that the wages fixed under the Minimum Wages Act, 1948 and are payable in cash. It also provides for payment of displacement allowance and journey allowance. The contractor has the liability to: (a) make regular payment of wages, ensuring equal pay for equal work irrespective of sex, (b) ensure suitable conditions of work, (c) provide and maintain suitable residential accommodation to such workmen during the period of their employment, (d) provide the prescribed medical facilities to the workmen free of charge, and (e) provide protective clothing to the workmen and in case of fatal accident or serious bodily injury to any such workman to report to the specified authorities of both the states and also the next-of-kin of the workman. The primary responsibility for payment of wages is on the contractor and on his failure on the principal employer.

5.7 Legal Aid Services

Guarantees of women's rights to equality can be realized only if women are encouraged to assert their rights in a court of law. In order to achieve this objective, there is need to ensure women's access to legal aid services. Article 39A of the

Constitution of India provides that State shall secure that the operation of the legal system promotes justice on a basis of equal opportunity, and shall in particular, provide free legal aid, by suitable legislation or schemes or in any other way, to ensure that opportunities for securing justice are not denied to any citizen by reason of economic or other disability. Articles 14 and 22(1) also make it obligatory for the State to ensure equality before law and a legal system which promotes justice on a basis of equal opportunity to all. Legal aid strives to ensure that constitutional pledge is fulfilled in its letter and spirit and equal justice is made available to the poor, downtrodden and weaker sections of the society.

5.7.1 Legal Services Authority Act, 1987: Section 12 of the Act includes women as a category eligible for free legal aid in its list of eligible persons. A nationwide network has been envisaged under the Act for providing legal aid and assistance. National Legal Services Authority is the apex body constituted to lay down policies and principles for making legal services available under the provisions of the Act and to frame most effective and economical schemes for legal services. It also disburses funds and grants to State Legal Services Authorities and NGOs for implementing legal aid schemes and programmes. It also envisages legal service authorities to be constituted at every state, district and taluk levels. These authorities are supposed to give effect to the policies, directions and implement legal aid schemes in their respective areas.

Legal aid to a woman however still remains a distant dream in India. Further, even if a woman decides to approach the court, she is beset with many hurdles like the quality of legal aid, attitude of the implementing bodies and the lengthy period of judicial process.

5.7.2 National Legal Research Desk (NLRD): The Constitution of India provides for special treatment of women, guarantees equality and prohibits discrimination. The Government of India has been strengthening various laws focused on women and children. This has been more visible since the Beijing CEDAW Conference. The recent years have been witness to some landmark interpretations and directives related to violence against women.

NLRD has been instituted to strengthen the implementation of the laws related to women and children in India. NLRD focuses on documenting the recent changes in the law, collects and compiles the recent landmark judgments of the Supreme Court of India and the High Courts and ensures a wider dissemination of the same through the government and the non-government machinery. NLRD works with law enforcement agencies, police academies, judicial agencies, government agencies, statutory agencies, NGOs, civil society and mass media on promoting access to justice for women and children. NLRD website is a knowledge hub for compilation of all laws, judgements and resource materials on violence against women and children in India. In the first phase, it focuses on laws related to human trafficking, domestic violence, juvenile justice, rape laws, honour crimes and victim compensation.

5.8 Implementation of Women-related Legislations

Though a large number of women-related legislations are in place, it is seen that the efficacy of these laws is not satisfactory primarily on account of poor implementation. A major reason for this is the lack of adequate knowledge regarding these special legislations and also absence of gender sensitivity on part of the functionaries such as police, prosecution, medical profession, judiciary etc. The Central and State Governments need to give a very high priority to training and capacity building of these stakeholders not only to educate them about the nuances of the laws but also to inculcate gender sensitivity in the system. The women themselves too need to be made aware of the special legislations that are available for their protection and rights. For this purpose, awareness generation and dissemination of information on a sustained basis is needed with special modules based on the region and group targets.

Thus, while there are a plethora of Acts existing for the protection and socio-economic equality of women, it is only through their effective implementation that women receive the intended benefits. However, gaps still remain and it is essential that specific laws are brought into effect which provide adequate safeguards and protection to women.

Despite the Constitutional mandate of equal legal status for men and women, the same is yet to be realized. The dejure laws have not been translated into *de facto* situation for various reasons such as illiteracy, social practices, prejudices, cultural norms based on patriarchal values, poor representation of women in policy making, poverty, regional disparity in development, lack of access and opportunity to information and resources etc. The ground situation more or less remains the same.

Most of the laws come with various institutional machineries, partnership between various stakeholders and active role of NGOs. These institutions need to be in existence in order for the law to be effective. Also the policies and programmes made at the top takes a long time to percolate to the bottom and there is an urgent need of sharing information and resources.

In an atmosphere like the present one, where the empowerment of women is endangered along with her dignity and integrity at stake, the only way out seems to be that of exclusive and strict legislations that bar further deterioration. This environment has thus given rise to certain segments of society who, *suo moto*, take charge to help victims and make way for change.

Poor implementation of women-specific legislations does not mean that the conditions of women workers have not undergone any change since the early days of industrialisation. In urban areas and particularly in large factories and establishments women have better conditions and many of the welfare provisions are implemented. However, in rural areas and amongst unorganised workers, much remains to be done.

Vigorous efforts by trade unions insisting on the enforcement of law and spreading legal literacy will go a long way towards improving the present conditions.

The awareness on laws and access to justice remains dismal. At the district and the state level, sensitivity on women rights among judicial officers, administration and the police is very low. This leads to a situation where the implementation of the law becomes difficult. Recently, India has increased its budgetary support for the implementation of various laws on violence against women and it becomes increasingly more important for the NGOs to work on governance, specially related to women and children issues.

6

Institutional Mechanism for Welfare of Women

Gender disparity manifests itself in various forms, the most obvious being the trend of continuously declining female ratio in the population in the last few decades. Social stereotyping and violence at the domestic and societal levels are some of the other manifestations. Discrimination against girl children, adolescent girls and women persists in parts of the country. The underlying causes of gender inequality are related to social and economic structure, which is based on informal and formal norms, and practices. Consequently, the access of women)—particularly those belonging to weaker sections including scheduled castes/scheduled tribes/other backward classes and minorities, majority of whom are in the rural areas and in the informal, unorganized sector)—to education, health and productive resources, among others, is inadequate. Therefore, they remain largely marginalized, poor and socially excluded.

Institutional mechanism for the advancement of women includes institutions of different types—Central, State and Local Governments, non-governmental organisations (NGOs), civil society and other bodies—which support the cause of women's advancement.

6.1 Structure of Institutional Set-up

Various institutional mechanisms that are contributing/will contribute to the achievement of women's empowerment and gender equality are as under.

1. Government structures with a mandate for women advancement such as Ministries, departments, focal points, bureaus, cells, desks, coordination units and committees, inter-agency committees etc.

2. The Parliamentary Committees on the Empowerment of Women.
3. Institutions of local government such as the three-tiered panchayats and urban local bodies which are to be delegated vast administrative, financial and legal powers across the development sectors, including social and women's development.
4. Mechanisms and plans such as gender budgets, component plans for women, action plans for women, monitoring and assessing instruments such as human development indices, audit systems such as gender and social audit, appraisals and evaluations using tools such as gender analysis, participatory exercises etc. To these can be added grassroots innovations capturing attention such as the *Jansunwais* (public hearings within an informal space) in the style of courts or other judicial bodies.
5. Women's bodies and groups working for the economic, social and political rights of women, all bearing the *voluntary* and *democratic* label, but with varying emphasis on different belief systems, ideologies and philosophies etc. ranging from academia, research, education, feminism, to action research and advocacy.
6. Federations, trade unions, cooperatives, youth and other age-based groups, ad-hoc groups formed for short-term objectives, watchdog bodies, local groups etc.

6.2 Ministry of Women and Child Development (MWCD)

The history of the present Ministry of Women and Child Development—the nodal agency for welfare, development and empowerment of women—is also the history of how women as a specific group were viewed by the successive Governments. The subject of women, prior to 1985, was dealt with by the Ministry of Social Welfare. In the year 1986, a separate Department for Women and Child Development was constituted under the aegis of Ministry of Human Resource Development, primarily keeping in mind that women were valuable human resources and therefore deserved more focused attention. This also implied a subtle shift from *welfare* to *development* approach for these sections. With effect from January 30, 2006 the Department was elevated to the status of a full-fledged independent Ministry, thus implicitly bringing issues related to women into the forefront with greater focus and a larger mandate. It also meant that the MWCD would enhance its commitment to women through wider range of programmatic interventions and outlays, advocate gender mainstreaming of other sectors.

Due to the wide-ranging facets and nuances of the nature of women' empowerment, the programmatic interventions perforce cannot be restricted to any one particular sector or Ministry/Department. The responsibility has to be shared between sectors and between Ministries/Departments with adequate scope for convergence and inter-sectoral linkages. Thus, the role of MWCD includes policy formulation, conception of innovative programmes and their implementation, coordination with other sectors and State Governments, gender budgeting, training and capacity building, monitoring the status of women and their rights. This requires that appropriate institutional mechanisms are in place both in the MWCD, other sectoral ministries and the State Governments so that implementation, networking, coordination and convergence is possible.

Thus, presently MWCD is the apex body for formulation and administration of the rules and regulations and laws relating to women and child development in India.

MWCD was constituted with the prime intention of addressing gaps in State action for women and children for promoting inter-Ministerial and inter-sectoral convergence to create gender equitable and child-centred legislation, policies and programmes.

6.2.1 Vision and Mission: The vision of MWCD has the objective of empowered women living with dignity and contributing as equal partners in development in an environment free from violence and discrimination. It also envisions well-nurtured children with full opportunities for growth and development in a safe and protective environment.

The mission of MWCD aims at promoting social and economic empowerment of women through cross-cuting policies and programmes, mainstreaming gender concerns, creating awareness about their rights and facilitating institutional and legislative support for enabling them realize their human rights and develop to their full potential. Ensuring development, care and protection of children through cross-cutting policies and programmes, spreading awareness about their rights and facilitating access to learning, nutrition, institutional and legislative support for enabling them to grow and develop to their full potential are some other goals.

6.2.2 Mandate: The broad mandate of MWCD is to have holistic development of women and children. As a nodal Ministry for the advancement of women and children, the Ministry formulates plans, policies and programmes; enacts/amends legislations, guides and co-ordinates the efforts of both governmental and non-governmental organisations working in the field of women and child development. Besides playing its nodal role, the Ministry implements certain innovative programmes for women and children. These programmes cover welfare and support services, training for employment and income generation, awareness generation and gender sensitization. These programmes play a supplementary and complementary role to the other general developmental programmes in the sectors of health, education, rural development etc. All these efforts are directed to ensure that women are empowered both economically and socially and thus become equal partners in national development along with men.

6.2.3 Policy Initiatives: For holistic development of the child, the Ministry has been implementing the world's largest outreach programme of Integrated Child Development Services (ICDS) providing a package of services comprising supplementary nutrition, immunization, health check-up and referral services, pre-school non-formal education. There is effective co-ordination and monitoring of various sectoral programmes. Most of the programmes of the Ministry are run through non-governmental organisations. Efforts are made to have more effective involvement of NGOs. The major policy initiatives undertaken by the Ministry in the recent past include universalisation of ICDS and *Kishori Shakti Yojana*, launching a nutrition programme for adolescent girls, establishment of the Commission for Protection of Child Rights and enactment of Protection of Women from Domestic Violence Act.

The ministry also gives the annual *Stree Shakti Puraskar* in six categories, namely Devi Ahilya Bai Holkar, Kannagi Award, Mata Jijabai Award, Rani Gaidinliu Zeliang Award, Rani Lakshmi Bai Award and Rani Rudramma Devi (for both men and women).

6.2.4 Organisation: The activities of the Ministry are undertaken through seven bureaux. The Ministry has 6 autonomous organisations working under its aegis.

- National Institute of Public Cooperation and Child Development (NIPCCD).
- National Commission for Women (NCW).
- National Commission for Protection of Child Rights (NCPCR).
- Central Adoption Resource Agency (CARA).
- Central Social Welfare Board (CSWB).
- Rashtriya Mahila Kosh (RMK).

NIPCCD and RMK are societies registered under the Societies Registration Act, 1860. CSWB is a charitable company registered under section 25 of the Indian Companies Act, 1956. These organisations are fully funded by the Government of India and they assist Ministry in its functions including implementation of some programmes/schemes. The National Commission for Women was constituted as a national apex statutory body in 1992 for protecting and safeguarding the rights of women. The National Commission for Protection of Child Rights which is a national level apex statutory body constituted in the March 2007 for protecting and safe guarding the rights of children.

6.2.5 Subjects Allocated: Subjects, *inter alia*, allocated to the Ministry are as under:

1. Integrated Child Protection Scheme.
2. Women and child welfare and co-ordination of activities of other Ministries and Organisations in connection with this subject.
3. References from the United Nations, National Nutrition Policy, National Plan of Action for Nutrition and National Nutrition Mission.
4. Charitable and religious endowments pertaining to subjects allocated to this Department.
5. Promotion and development of voluntary effort on the subjects allocated to this Department.
6. Co-ordination of activities of Cooperative for Assistance and Relief Everywhere (CARE).
7. Planning, research, evaluation, monitoring, project formulations, statistics and training relating to the welfare and development of women and children, including development of gender sensitive data base.
8. United Nations Children's Fund (UNICEF).
9. Central Social Welfare Board (CSWB).
10. National Institute of Public Cooperation and Child Development (NIPCCD).
11. Food and Nutrition Board (FNB).
12. Development and popularization of subsidiary and protective foods.
13. Nutrition extension.
14. Women's empowerment and gender equity.
15. National Commission for Women.
16. Rashtriya Mahila Kosh (RMK).
17. Implementation of:

- Immoral Traffic in Women and Girl Act, 1956 (as amended up to 1986).
- Indecent Representation of Women (Prevention) Act, 1986.

- Dowry Prohibition Act, 1961.
- Commission of Sati (Prevention) Act, 1987, excluding the administration of criminal justice in regard to offences under these Acts.
- Infant Milk Substitutes, Feeding Bottles and Infant Food (Regulation of Production, Supply and Distribution) Act, 1992.
- Juvenile Justice (Care and Protection of Children) Act, 2000.
- Children Act, 1960.
- Child Marriage Restraint Act, 1929.

6.3 Autonomous Organisations under MWCD

MWCD has the following 4 autonomous organizations working under its aegis:

1. National Institute of Public Co-operation and Child Development (NIPCCD).
2. Rashtriya Mahila Kosh (RMK).
3. Central Social Welfare Board (CSWB).
4. Central Adoption Resource Agency (CARA).

NIPCCD, RMK and CARA are societies registered under the Societies Registration Act, 1860. CSWB is a charitable company registered under section 25 of the Indian Companies Act, 1956. These organizations are fully funded by the Government of India and they assist the Ministry in its functions including implementation of programmes/schemes.

In addition to these, National Commission for Women was constituted as a national apex statutory body in 1992 for protecting and safeguarding the rights of women. Similarly, National Commission for Protection of Child Rights (NCPCR) was set up in 2007 to protect and safeguard the rights of children.

6.3.1 National Institute of Public Co-operation and Child Development (NIPCCD): NIPCCD is a successor to the Central Institute of Research and Training in Public Cooperation which was sponsored by the Planning Commission and registered under the Societies Registration Act, 1860 as an autonomous organisation on February 28, 1966. NIPCCD functions under the aegis of the Department of Women and Child Development with its Headquarters in New Delhi.

The objectives of NIPCCD are to: (a) develop and promote voluntary action in social development, (b) take a comprehensive view of child development and develop and promote programmes in pursuance of the National Policy for Children, (c) develop measures for coordination of governmental and voluntary action in social development, and (d) evolve framework and perspective for organising children's programmes through governmental and voluntary efforts.

With a view to achieving the above objectives, NIPCCD: (a) organises training programmes, seminars, workshops, conferences, (b) conducts research and evaluation studies, and (c) provides documentation and information services in the field of public cooperation and child development. NIPCCD is the apex body for training of functionaries of the Integrated Child Development Services (ICDS) programme. It provides technical advice and consultancy to government and voluntary agencies in promoting and implementing policies and programmes for child development and voluntary action. In addition, it collaborates with regional and international agencies, research institutions, universities and technical bodies.

6.3.2 Rashtriya Mahila Kosh (RMK): RMK was established in 1993 to provide micro credit in a quasi-formal manner to the poor women for income generating, production, skill development and housing activities in order to make them economically independent. RMK mainly channelises its support through NGOs, voluntary agencies, state women development corporations, cooperative societies, state government agencies, urban women co-operative banks etc. to women SHGs. It is an innovative mechanism for extending credit to poor women. Through access to credit, it aims to raise the capacity of women by enhancing through productivity and economic self-reliance.

6.3.3 Central Social Welfare Board (CSWB): CSWB was set up on August 12, 1953 by a Resolution of Government of India to act as an apex body at national level for welfare and development of women and children. State Social Welfare Boards were established in 1954 in all State capitals to support CSWB in achieving its objectives.

6.3.4 Central Adoption Resource Agency (CARA): CARA has initiated various steps for the promotion of in-country adoption. These include strengthening the Voluntary Coordinating Agencies (VCAs) by providing them grants-in-aid.

6.3.5 National Commission for Women (NCW): NCW was set up in 1992 to protect and safeguard the rights of women. The activities of the Commission include receiving complaints or suo moto enquiring in cases of deprivation of rights of women, providing counselling, conducting *Parivarik Lok Adalats* and legal awareness programmes and organising public hearings.

NCW being the nodal agency for protection of the rights of women needs to be strengthened. The NCW Act needs to be suitably amended to give the Commission more power.

NCW, a statutory body, set up under the National Commission for Women Act, 1990, has a mandate to safeguard the rights and interests of women. The Commission pursues its mandated activities, namely review of laws, interventions into specific individual complaints of atrocities and remedial action to safeguard the interests of women, whatever appropriate and feasible. The Commission has accorded highest priority to securing speedy justice for women.

The Commission has been instrumental in introducing fresh ideas, innovative model, training, packages, model for speedy justice etc. The Commission has, before it, apart from looking into the laws and legislations for effecting improvement to ensure speedy justice, has focussed on thrust areas in the realm of:

1. Organising through NGOs *Parivarik Mahila Lok Adalats*

throughout the length and breadth of the country on a continuous basis;
2. Launching of programmes on legal awareness;
3. Sensitisation programmes for police, NGOs, officials for better implementation of safeguards and laws for the benefit of women;
4. Release and rehabilitation of women prisoners;
5. Rehabilitation of prostitutes and their children;
6. Rehabilitation of widows and land support to anti arrack movement;
7. Custodial justice for women prisoners;
8. Participation of women in the electoral process;
9. Issue of violence on women;
10. *Dahej Mukti Abhiyan*;
11. Technological empowerment of women in agriculture; and
12. Rights of minority women.

The Commission maintains the complaints cell/counselling cell which is a core unit of the Commission and processes various categories of written/oral complaints and also take suo-moto notice of matters relating to deprivation of women's rights, non-implementation of laws enacted to provide protection to women, non-compliance of policy decisions, guidelines or instructions aimed at mitigating hardships to women and taking up issues arising out of such matters with appropriate authorities. The complaints received relate to harassment for dowry, dowry deaths, torture, desertion, bigamy, rape, refusal to register FIR by the police, discrimination in employment, domestic violence, incest and cruelty by husbands and in-laws.

6.3.6 National Commission for Protection of Child Rights (NCPCR): As envisaged in the Commission for Protection of Child Rights Act 2005, notified in the Gazette of India on January 20, 2006 as Act No. 4 of 2006, the Government set up NCPCR with effect from March 5, 2007.

In short, women's movements and a widespread network of non-government organisations (NGOs)—which have strong grassroots presence and deep insight into women's concerns)—have contributed in inspiring initiatives for the empowerment of women. However, there still exists a wide gap between the goals enunciated in the Constitution, legislations, policies, plans, programmes and related mechanisms on the one hand and the situational reality of the status of women in India, on the other.

The Ministry of Women and Child Development, as the nodal agency for all matters pertaining to welfare, development and empowerment of women, has evolved schemes and programmes for their benefit. These schemes are spread across a broader spectrum such as women's need for shelter, security, safety, legal aid, justice, information, maternal health, food, nutrition etc. as well as their need for economic sustenance through skill development, education, and access to credit and marketing.

7

Economic Empowerment of Women

If society is serious about substantially improving the economic status of poor women working in the informal sector of the economy, it has to devise concrete strategies, which can help to enhance the ownership of and control over productive assets of these women. Perhaps it will be the single most important intervention towards both their empowerment and economic well-being. Some of the assets that women can be given are a plot of land housing, tree *pattas*, joint ownership of all assets transferred by the State to the family, livestock license, bank accounts, membership of organizations and identity cards.

7.1 Vicious Circle of Poverty and Gender Inequality

Poverty and gender inequality thrive on each other. In other words, there exists a two-way link between economic growth and poverty, and gender inequality. At one level, poverty and the lack of growth exacerbate gender disparities. Inequalities between girls and boys in access to schooling or adequate health care are more acute among poor people than among those with higher incomes. While poor people have less access to such productive resources as land and credit, poor women generally have the least access of all. Similarly, health and schooling of girls and women are more vulnerable to economic downturns than those of boys and men. At another level, gender inequalities undermine the prospects for poverty reduction in fundamental ways. While disparities in basic rights, access to schooling, credit and jobs, and the ability to participate in public life take their most direct toll on women and girls, the evidence shows that gender inequality ultimately hinders economic growth.

The rationale for economically empowering women is compelling both for its own sake and for other spill over benefits. Economic participation of women—their presence in the workforce in quantitative terms—is important not only for lowering the disproportionate levels of poverty among women, but also as an important step toward raising household income and encouraging economic development in a country. Education, employment and ownership rights of women have a powerful influence on their ability to control their environment and contribute to economic development.

However, participation alone is not enough because quality of women's work is also important. A key challenge is to overcome a situation where women may gain employment with relative ease, but where their employment is either concentrated in poorly paid or *unskilled job ghettos*, characterized by the absence of upward mobility and opportunity. For example, women are often concentrated in *feminized professions* such as nursing and teaching, office work, care of the elderly and disabled—termed *horizontal occupational segregation*—where they tend to remain in lower job categories than men. Since these activities are carried out by women, they are the lowest paid, in addition to offering limited or no opportunity for advancement. The term *feminization of poverty* is often used to illustrate the fact that a substantial percentage of poor are women and that the gap between women and men in poverty has not lessened, but may well have widened in recent years.

7.2 Gender-sensitive Macroeconomic Policies

Gender inequalities manifest as women and men have different access to resources, roles and responsibilities, both in the market and at the household. In the Indian context, fiscal policies are being increasingly examined through gender sensitive-budgeting exercises, although the focus still remains on expenditures in *soft sectors*, with several aspects like taxation, trade, capital flows etc. remaining largely an unstudied domain. Macroeconomic policies are formulated and implemented in areas such as trade, fiscal management, debt financing, social welfare and other sectors without a comprehensive assessment of their potential gender impacts. All these issues would be particularly important if the analysis of the sources of growth were to suggest that influencing the distribution of income and assets by gender might have a beneficial effect. Some policies—particularly those promoting health and education, or promoting greater women's property rights and control over assets or access to credit, technology, and transport—are likely to be win-win policies in terms of higher growth, greater gender equality, and reduced susceptibility of women to economic shock.

7.3 Gender-responsive Infrastructure

Development of infrastructure was previously assumed to be gender neutral, with both sexes benefiting equally from well-designed projects. The new thinking asserts that gender-responsive infrastructure interventions can free up women's time, thereby increasing girls' enrolment in schools and facilitating women's participation in income-generation and decision-making activities.

7.3.1 Transport: In the area of transport, men and women have varying transport needs and constraints and are affected differently by transport interventions. Rural transport projects that build roads for motorized transport often do not benefit rural women, who mainly work in and around the village and travel on foot. Urban transport systems that transport people to and from employment centres are sometimes inadequate for women, who must combine income-generating activities with household and familial activities, such as taking children to school and health centres and visiting the market. Poor women, who balance productive, social, and reproductive roles in societies, often have higher demands on their time than poor men.

There are women-specific transport needs like transportation of primary products; inter- and intra-village roads/paths; non-motorised transport; dedicated bicycle lanes, pedestrian sidewalk use, passenger safety, and so on which should be included in any transport policy or plan. Every major transport project should undertake a pre-project gender assessment survey to ensure that women's needs are addressed right at the design and planning level. Project planning and implementation need to be participatory, including community infrastructure management and maintenance.

Design improvements are necessary to meet the specific needs of women, especially lower height of entry steps, length of straps, and so on in buses and trains, installation of handrails, ramps, and so on. Dedicated exclusive services such as ladies special buses and trains are also necessary. Women's needs require better route planning. The provision of special buses, increased services for women travelling during off-peak hours or services on less-travelled routes all need more attention. Personal security risks at parking lots, buses, bus stops, airports, highways etc. A gender audit of transport terminals must be undertaken and safety measures for women introduced.

7.3.2 Energy: Women are disproportionately impacted by a lack of access to energy given their prominent role in domestic, low paid and unpaid work. In rural India women spend considerable time in gathering fuels and processing them, i.e. chopping, drying, turning, storing, stacking and handling. This work is done almost exclusively by women. Since this energy system is managed by women, they need to be substantially supported through investment, management and technology inputs to be able to continue to manage the systems in sustainable ways and with minimum hardship. Thus, the focus should be not only on meeting cooking energy needs but also on enhanced livelihood options. Both rural and urban women need adequate energy supplies for their small and medium scale enterprises and home industries. Hence, there is a commercial motivation to improve the efficiency of the entire process.

7.3.3 Information and Communication Technology (ICT): ICT has delivered enormous benefits around the world. However, much of their potential remains untapped—particularly for groups facing severe time constraints, suffering from social isolation, or lacking access to knowledge and productive resources. Women in developing countries are among the most important of these groups. Although women account for nearly a third of information technology workers in developing countries, they are concentrated in lower-level jobs (data entry, call centres etc.) and paid smaller salaries than men. Few are project managers. With supportive policies from employers, complemented by enlightened national labour laws, women can move up the professional ladder. Low enrolment of girls and women in science and technology education is one of the main obstacles to higher level employment in information technology.

In India, where software services are major exports, women have been targeted by government initiatives promoting the growth of the ICT workforce. Supported by gender-sensitive human resource development policies and training strategies, women in India are being trained to provide basic services such as data processing. They are also encouraged to develop their skills in order to go beyond back-office work and become website designers, network managers or ICT service consultants. The idea is to make them suitable for enhanced work opportunities, on equal terms with men. It is worth mentioning here that certain software companies offer crèche facilities to working women.

7.4 Gender-sensitive Agricultural Policies

Rural women form the most important productive work force in the Indian economy. Beyond the conventional market-oriented narrower definition of *productive workers*, almost all women in rural India can be considered as *farmers* in some sense, working as agricultural labourers, unpaid workers in the family farm enterprise, or combination of the two. Moreover, several farm activities traditionally carried out by men are also being undertaken by women as men are pulled away into higher paying employment. Thus, rural India is witnessing a process which could be described as feminization of agriculture.

Despite significant contribution of women in the production process, an all pervasive bias of development planners in treating them primarily as consumers of social services rather than producers, kept them away from the development programmes in agriculture and allied sectors. As men and women have different roles and needs and face gender-specific constraints, women may not automatically benefit from development activities, but may remain excluded.

In spite of the key role of women in crop husbandry, animal husbandry, fisheries, forestry and post-harvest technology, those in-charge of formulating packages of technologies, services and public policies for rural areas have often tended to neglect the productive role of women. Consequently, the developments of technologies, specifically tailored to women-specific occupations and the involvement of women in technology development and transfer have received inadequate attention from both scientific and administrative departments of Government.

Women have traditionally been discriminated in their access to productive resources and have been denied ownership of land, cattle, trees, harvest and shelter. They have even been discriminated in access to credit and marketing facilities for their economic activities. It is, thus, essential to develop strategies and mechanism to improve women's access to agricultural support services.

It has been recognized that for an accelerated socio-economic development of any community, the active participation of women in the entire process is very essential. In a social set up like ours, the participation of women in the development process has to be ensured through tangible measures, taken at various levels, which result in empowerment of women in the real sense. In view of the above, government has taken a conscious view to make adequate provisions in its policies and programmes through which it is to be ensured that the women of the country are empowered and they become the active participants in the development process.

The absence of faster diversification is partly due to the lack of new economic opportunities for women. While men migrate as well as take up new employment opportunities in rural areas, women find themselves at a disadvantage.

There appears to be a faster rate of occupational mobility out of agriculture among men than among women. The latter remain more bound to rural areas and to agriculture due to socio-cultural and structural causes.

7.4.1 Importance of Land for Women: Land is important for women due to following reasons:

1. Land access can reduce a household's risk of poverty, but for persistent gender inequalities land solely in men's hands need not guarantee female welfare.
2. Direct land transfers to women are likely to benefit not just women but also children. Evidence, both from India and from many other parts of the world, shows that women, especially in poor households, spend most of the earnings they control on basic household needs, while men spend a significant part of theirs on personal goods, such as alcohol, tobacco etc.
3. Women with assets such as land have greater bargaining power, which can lead to more gender-equal allocations of benefits even from male incomes.
4. Women without independent resources are highly vulnerable to poverty and destitution in case of desertion, divorce, or widowhood. In parts of western and north-western India, rural women even from rich parental and marital families, deprived of their property shares when widowed, can be found working as agricultural labourers

on the farms of their well-off brothers or brothers-in-law. The fate of deserted and divorced women is worse.

5. Tenure security, and especially titles, can empower women to assert themselves better with agencies that provide inputs and extension services.
6. Women in many parts of South Asia are often better informed than men about traditional seed varieties and the attributes of trees and grasses. If they have greater control over land and farming, this knowledge can be put to better use.

7.4.2 Sources of Land for Women: There are three main sources of land for women:

1. Direct government transfers.
2. Market purchase/lease.
3. Inheritance or gifts from families.

To enhance women's land access from all three sources, a range of initiatives are needed, including land titles to women in all government land transfers, credit support to poor women to purchase or lease in land from the market, raising legal awareness and legal support about women's inheritance rights.

It will also need a new approach to enable women to retain the land they get by strongly encouraging a *group approach* in land cultivation and investment in productive assets. It is now well-recognized that the poor are best empowered if they function as a group rather than as individuals. This lesson should be incorporated in the creation of all productive assets in women's hands.

Agricultural policies are of prime importance in gender budgeting exercises as there is a growing feminization of agriculture in recent years with out-migration of men to urban areas in search of work. The number of women-headed households in the agricultural sector is also increasing. The prosperity of agriculture therefore will largely depend on how effectively these women are empowered.

Enhancing women's rights to land, providing infrastructure support to women farmers and advancing legal support on existing laws are some of the policy interventions needed. However, critical problems persist. The lack of formal titles to women on the land they cultivate is a big drawback. This adversely affects their access to credit, inputs and marketing outlets. It also reinforces women's position as unpaid farm labourers, which reduces their incentives to invest in the land. It further excludes them from receiving agricultural extension services, new production techniques etc.

The lack of appropriate women-friendly tools and agricultural implements is another drawback. Also, the co-operatives of farmers basically comprise of men and therefore disadvantageous to women in terms of mindset and location and services profile. The agricultural policy, therefore, needs to be reviewed to provide a gender-friendly perspective.

Policies for non-farm sector and information are another highly important area that has to be seriously reviewed keeping in view the gender perspective. As women tend to remain in the rural sector, they also undertake non-farm activities, which significantly contribute to the family's income. In times of agricultural stress, it is these non-farm activities of women that support the family. Therefore, the requirements of women in this sector need to be identified and appropriate support facilities in terms of access to raw materials, micro credit, skill development, training, market linkages etc. have to be ensured.

7.5 Gender-Sensitive Resettlement and Rehabilitation Policy

The process of involuntary resettlement as a result of large development projects often leads to loss of land, wage employment, and housing and shelter, calling for gender-sensitive plans toward land-based re-settlement, re-employment and re-construction of houses. For instance, women should also get legal rights to land allocated as part of a resettlement package. Women's livelihood and economic activities—be they gathering forest produce, working in the fields or selling agricultural, animal husbandry, forestry or fishery produce—need to be enumerated so that the resettlement and rehabilitation plan also makes provision for the restoration of their livelihood and income. Women's views need to be solicited regarding houses, toilets, water and sanitation.

The process of displacement and involuntary resettlement also leads to increased stress, psychological trauma, increasing exposure to parasitic and vector-borne diseases and to social evils and violence. Endemic infections may lead to the death of children and the elderly in the care of women. Alcoholism, gambling and prostitution and increase in the incidence of sexual abuse and violence as a result of large-scale dislocation of peoples adversely affect women in ways different from that of men. Involuntary resettlement also increases the risk that the affected household may fall into chronic food insecurity. Loss of common property resources (CPRs) like access to forests, water bodies and grazing lands are often disregarded by planners and are not compensated for.

Loss of CPRs leads to women spending more time and energy accessing fuel, fodder and potable water. Involuntary resettlement also leads to loss of social status as a result of loss of community networks and social marginalisation. Women are affected, more deeply and differently than men, because they generally have lower levels of skills and education and have a limited social exposure. Women rely on community networks for emotional and practical support, for example, taking care of the children, and thus the dislocation of community networks can be traumatic for them. Community services and assets need to be restored and social networks and communities need to be rebuilt in consultation and with the active participation of women.

The fact that the impact of dislocation is different for women needs to be understood and mitigated. Also, in drawing up resettlement and rehabilitation plans, care should be taken to see that widows, elderly persons, divorced women and women-headed households do not suffer a loss of their rights as a result of patriarchal biases. Detailed studies of the impact of development projects, say large dams, on women's lives, especially regarding resettlement and rehabilitation need to be sponsored, which can then be used to formulate a gender-sensitive resettlement and rehabilitation policy. The issue of a gender-sensitive resettlement and rehabilitation policy has not been addressed and this deserves immediate public attention.

7.6 Self-help Groups (SHGs) for Women

The emergence and rapid multiplication of self-help groups (SHGs) based on micro credit is a phenomenon that is gaining increasing importance in the development scenario. SHGs are being viewed by governments and NGOs as a strategy for both women's empowerment as well as poverty reduction. SHGs are a conduit for routing a wide range of government-sponsored development messages and schemes. NGOs have increasingly been adopting SHGs as a strategy to bring women together, at a faster pace and larger scale than the collective building processes adopted by them earlier. A number of powerful players like MFIs, NGOs, corporations and donors—all of whom have a significant and growing interest in the SHG phenomenon which centres on poor women—have entered the arena. Credit is a right that poor women must have access to.

The experience of SHGs has shown that they have provided improved access to credit. Poor women are now perceived by the mainstream financial sector as creditworthy. Women have used savings and credit for needs such as those related to education and health, and in particular for crisis related needs. Participation in SHGs has meant opportunities related to mobility and a legitimate space in the public realm for leaders of SHGs. Notwithstanding all the positive achievements, the overall picture is uneven and raises following concerns related to gender justice and livelihoods:

1. Despite the increased access to credit, there continue to be several hurdles faced by women when they want to access credit from banks. These include huge amounts of

paperwork and the fact that women are often pressurized by banks to recover loans made earlier to men in the village as an unwritten conditionality before loans are released to them.

2. It is increasingly being reported that SHG members have limited control over financial resources that they borrow despite being the conduit for access to such credit through their groups. The burden of repayment of such loans falls almost exclusively on the women. As SHGs are almost exclusively women-only, often women become proxy to husband's demands without the men taking up the responsibility for repayment or proper utilization of these loans.
3. Many of the micro enterprise activities undertaken have tended to be unviable. Low levels of credit absorption capacity, low skill base and low asset base have been challenges to the SHG movement, which are yet to be addressed. Moreover, lack of skills, experience and technical support services to promote livelihoods and build sustainable interventions among the intermediary organizations especially NGOs etc. does not enable sustainable livelihood options to be developed.
4. Access to credit as the focus of the micro credit programmes looses sight of the fundamental issues of access and control over common resources such as water forests etc which are the mainstay of occupations of a large number of the rural poor. The fundamental livelihood concerns related to the existing economic realities of poor women's lives remain largely unaddressed in the process.

7.7 Skill Development

With the advent of globalisation and liberalization, new technologies and fast changing markets tend to make existing skills obsolete, requiring upgradation of existing skills and adoption of new skills and multi-skilling. Globalisation often puts a premium on skills, requiring high levels of education, often out of the reach of the unorganised sector workers. On the other hand, it opens up new markets which workers can reach by adopting existing or traditional skills.

Women workers are usually at the lowest-paid end of any sector. They are usually termed as unskilled, even though very often their work, though low-paid, requires a certain level of technique. Furthermore, many of the skills that women learn are those that are in some way connected to care and reproduction, which are often not regarded as skills at all. For example, women in forest areas have a skill of recognizing and using herbal plants. However, this skill is not regarded as skill at all, either by the person who is documenting the skills, or even by the women themselves.

Similarly, the potential marketability of a particular skill is never recognized. This refers to a woman's skills which currently are not being marketed but which have a good market potential like embroidery or knowledge of herbs. The *care skills* of the women can no longer be sidelined. These would include knowledge of child-care, care of the sick and particular skills such as mid-wifery. One unfortunate tendency that has been noticed in the desperate search for employment that goes on in the unorganised sector is the tendency towards deskilling. Workers lose their traditional or acquired skills when they cannot find employment with these skills.

7.8 Gender Mainstreaming in the Corporate Sector

While so far the focus of gender budgeting has been on public expenditure of Government only, an increasing quantum of funds is being invested by the corporate sector in their businesses as well as in fulfilling their corporate social responsibility. The development of the corporate sector as an employer has grown tremendously in the wake of liberalization and globalization, especially with its entry in those sectors which were hitherto the domain of the Government. Therefore, the time has come to apply the strategy of gender budgeting to the private sector. There is a three-fold responsibility that rests with the corporate sector:

1. Extending the scope of employment opportunities to more and more women.
2. Providing them with level playing fields (equal wages and promotion opportunities).
3. Supporting skill building, training, vocational courses etc.
4. Fulfilling social obligations towards women employees in terms of: (a) extending maternity benefits, (b) protection from occupational hazards and sexual harassment, (c) provision of facilities like crèches, toilets, sanitation and hygiene, (d) allowing formation of women's associations and (e) legal protection etc.

The civil society organizations whether NGOs or other community-based organizations are partnering with government in formulation and implementation of government policies and programmes. Thus, their voice and views have an important bearing on shaping economic or social issues pertaining to women. They have to function as *watchdogs* ensuring that gender budgeting and mainstreaming is actually taking place right at the grassroots levels and helping in implementing gender concerns effectively.

In order to address the developmental issues relating to women, a Task Force on Women and Children (Chairman: K.C. Pant) was constituted by the Government in August 2000. In its report submitted in April 2002, the Task Force, *inter alia*, recommended the setting up of an Inter-Ministerial Standing Committee in the Department of Women and Child Development, composed of officials and non-official experts to review and monitor gender mainstreaming in government. The Task Force also reviewed the whole gamut of legislations concerning women and recommended amendment of 22 laws to make them more effective.

7.9 Gender-friendly Insurance Schemes

The possibilities of gender differentials for social security *insurance* schemes is another area that needs to be examined, as there is an urgent need for low-cost and gender-friendly insurance systems that cater to the specific life cycle needs of women. It must be acknowledged that a safety net/social security in the informal sector is almost non-existent. As women comprise a large proportion of the informal sector, this implies that they are excluded from the insurance framework and therefore not protected against social, medical or economic emergencies. More importantly, it is absolutely necessary to put in place a well-designed health insurance scheme for women in view of their inability to access medical facilities. Also pension policies need a relook in view of the large number of widow population in the country.

7.10 Gender Sensitization of Trade Policy

United Nations Conference on Trade and Development (UNCTAD) organized an International Conference on Moving towards Gender Sensitization of Trade Policy in New Delhi from February 25 to 27, 2008.

The Conference provided a forum for Indian and international trade and gender experts to discuss and raise awareness on trade performance and gender linkages in India and globally and propose actions and directions towards enhanced and more effective gender sensitisation of trade policy with particular reference to India and generally to developing countries.

Equitable distribution of gains from trade among the genders is a development objective which needs to be addressed through trade policies and trade agreements. Women are significant stakeholders in the process of trade, growth and development. This must be recognized and harnessed by Government to make globalization more inclusive with pro-poor impact. Women groups must be consulted to a greater extent and in a systematic and structured manner, in the formulation of trade policies or negotiating positions, so as to integrate the gender dimension, he suggested.

Broadly, the Conference deliberations suggested a strong

and direct relationship between trade performance, gender empowerment and development, explicit and specific attention to gender issues in policy and operational actions, as well as in attitudes, which are key conditions for maximizing the gains for gender empowerment through trade and minimizing the costs that can arise. This is important because overall the situation in India and in many developing countries presently is that there is progress towards gender empowerment through trade. Moreover, a gender-sensitive approach to trade must involve a vision of trade as an integral component of wider development efforts to eradicate poverty and promote inclusive, people-centred development.

7.11 Right to Maintenance

Maintenance is a civil right that enables needy persons to receive economic support from those who are liable to protect and maintain their spouse, children, parents etc. By law, parents are bound to maintain minor children, major children their parents, husband his wife and vice versa. The quantum of maintenance varies depending on the economic status of the parties. The various personal laws such as the Hindu Marriage Act, 1955, the Hindu Adoption and Maintenance Act, 1955, the Indian Divorce Act, 1859, the Parsi Marriage Act, 1954, the Shariat Laws etc. provide for maintenance, also known as alimony or allowance. Civil courts take a long time to dispose off cases. Even if a competent civil court passes a judgement and decree, execution takes months and even years due to cumbersome legal procedures. Even before the maintenance is realised the decree holder may die of starvation.

Realising the above, the right to maintenance has been incorporated in Chapter IX of the Criminal Procedure Code (Cr.P.C.). It is entitled 'order for maintenance of Wives, Children and Parents'. Under Section 125 of the Cr.P.C., 'if any person having sufficient means neglects to maintain: (a) his wife, unable to maintain herself, or (b) his legitimate or illegitimate minor child, whether married or not, unable to maintain itself, or (c) his legitimate or illegitimate child (not being married) who has attained majority, where such child is, by reason of any physical or mental abnormality or injury unable to maintain itself, or (d) his father or mother, unable to maintain himself or herself, a magistrate, of the first class, may upon proof of such neglect or refusal, order such person to make a monthly allowance for the maintenance of his wife or such monthly rate not exceeding ₹ 500 on the whole, as the magistrate thinks fit, and to pay the same to such person as the magistrate may from time to time direct'.

A ceiling of ₹ 500 per month towards maintenance will not prevent vagrancy though that is the object of the provision. Various women and civil rights organizations and other activists have raised their voice against this ceiling. In West Bengal, the amount was raised to ₹ 1,500. Through an amendment to Section 125 of the Cr.P.C, the Government of India enhanced the interim maintenance limit for an estranged wife from ₹ 500 to ₹ 5,000.

7.12 Building Community Support

People do not live in isolation. They are surrounded by the family, health workers, teachers, community and religious leaders, NGOs etc. All these people may have different perceptions, needs, attitudes and preferences, with varying levels of awareness and sensitivity to gender issues. Moreover, these sections continuously interact with one another to produce the dominant norms, values and ideals of society. In this particular context, the needs, aspirations, and problems of a specific population are to be dealt with. Primarily, their attitudes and values have to be taken into consideration. For instance, in the case of women in the slums, it may not be possible to effectively intervene if they do not have information on income generating avenues, guidance or support from government departments, or if the community does not support them in activities or programmes they are participating in.

Also, it needs to be recognised that different sections of the community may have comparative advantage over the others in one or more spheres such as information, resources, skills or knowledge. Experienced NGOs or health services can perhaps provide the best technical information and services. Religious leaders may have the highest moral authority.

Community leaders can provide support and credibility to programmes and women may need the support of their families. Forging partnerships between these sections of the community for growth and change in the traditional attitudes and norms becomes essential. It is through the support of these partnerships that the needs and aspirations can be fulfilled and the community gender sensitised.

An integrated approach targets immediate needs through short-term strategies in the context of long-term needs in targeting social change. Studies have shown that communities are responsive to change when it is backed by information, skills and opportunities.

7.13 Rajiv Gandhi Scheme for Empowerment of Adolescent Girls (RGSEAG)—Sabla

This scheme was launched on November 19, 2010 with the objective of empowering adolescent girls in the age group 11-18 years by bringing improvement in their nutritional and health status and upgrading various skills like home skills, life skills, and vocational skills. To start with, it will be implemented in 200 selected districts across the country on a pilot basis. RGSEAG would be implemented through State Governments/UT Administrations with 100 percent financial assistance from the Central Government for all inputs other than nutrition provision for which 50 percent Central assistance to states/UTs would be provided. Anganwadi centres will be the focal points for delivery of services. Nearly 100 lakh adolescent girls in 200 districts are expected to be benefited per annum under the scheme. In these 200 districts, Kishori Shakti Yojna (KSY) and the Nutrition Programme for Adolescent Girls (NPAG) have been merged in the RGSEAG.

In the remaining districts, the KSY will continue as before.

7.14 Working Women Hostels

It is a scheme to provide safe and affordable accommodation to working women.

With the progressive change in the socio-economic fabric of the country, more and more women are leaving their homes in search of employment in big cities as well as urban and rural industrial clusters. One of the main difficulties faced by such women is lack of safe and conveniently located accommodation. The Government of India being concerned about the difficulties faced by such working women, introduced a scheme in 1972-73 of grant-in-aid for construction of new/expansion of existing buildings for providing hostel facilities to working women in cities, smaller towns and also in rural areas where employment opportunities for women exist. Based on an evaluation, the existing scheme was revised to promote availability of safe and conveniently located accommodation for working women who need to live away from their families due to professional commitments.

The objective of the scheme is to promote availability of safe and conveniently located accommodation for working women, with day care facility for their children, wherever possible, in urban, semi urban, or even rural areas where employment opportunity for women exist. To achieve this objective, the scheme assists projects for construction of new hostel buildings, expansion of existing hostel buildings and hostel buildings in rented premises. The working women's hostel projects being assisted under this scheme shall be made available to all working women without any distinction with respect to caste, religion, marital status etc., subject to norms prescribed under the scheme. While the projects assisted under this scheme are meant for working women, women under training for job may also be accommodated in such hostels subject to the condition that taken together, such trainees should not occupy more than 30 percent of the total capacity the hostel and they may be accommodated in the hostels only when adequate numbers of working women are not available. Children of working women, up to the age of 18 years for girls and up to the age of 5 years for boys may be accommodated in such hostel with their mothers.

7.15 Swadhar Greh

It is a scheme which caters to primary needs of women in difficult circumstances. It subsumed two earlier similar schemes, namely Short Stay Home scheme and Swadhar scheme.

Recognizing the need to prevent women from exploitation and to support their survival and rehabilitation, the scheme of Short Stay Home for women and girls was introduced as a social defence mechanism by the then Department of Social Welfare in 1969. The scheme is meant to provide temporary accommodation, maintenance and rehabilitative services to women and girls rendered homeless due to family discord, crime, violence, mental stress, social ostracism or are being forced into prostitution and are in moral danger. Another scheme with the similar objectives, namely Swadhar (a scheme for women in difficult circumstances) was launched in 2001-02. An evaluation study was conducted in 2007 to assess the performance of both the schemes.

The evaluation report while citing the effectiveness and positive impact of measures adopted under the schemes for counselling and rehabilitation found that the profile and category of residents, admission procedure, counselling, quality of service, vocational training, rehabilitation and follow up procedure are almost similar in both the schemes. It, therefore, recommended merger of these two schemes for better functioning and outcomes with lesser administrative burdens and procedures. It also recommended that the new scheme should focus on establishing one such home in every district. The positive findings of the evaluation study encouraged the Government to propose this new scheme that would target the women victims of unfortunate circumstances who are in need of institutional support for rehabilitation so that they could lead their life with dignity.

The scheme envisions a supportive institutional framework for women victims of difficult circumstances so that they could lead their life with dignity and conviction. It envisages that shelter, food, clothing, and health as well as economic and social security are assured for such women. It also envisions that the special needs of these women are properly taken care of and under no circumstances they should be left unattended or abandoned which could lead to their exploitation and desolation.

7.16 Compensation to Rape Victims

The Supreme Court in *Delhi Domestic Working Women's Forum vs. Union of India and Others* writ petition (CRL) No. 362/93 had directed the National Commission for Women to evolve a "scheme so as to wipe out the tears of unfortunate victims of rape". The Supreme Court observed that having regard to the Directive principles contained in the Article 38(1) of the Constitution, it was necessary to set up Criminal Injuries Compensation Board, as rape victims besides the mental anguish, frequently incur substantial financial loss and in some cases are too traumatized to continue in employment.

The Court further directed that compensation for victims shall be awarded by the Court on conviction of the offender and by the Criminal Injuries Compensation Board whether or not a conviction has taken place. The Board shall take into account pain, suffering and shock as well as loss of earnings due to pregnancy and the expenses of child birth if this occurs as a result of rape. Accordingly, NCW has drafted a scheme titled "Relief to and Rehabilitation of Rape Victims".

To sum up, the overall picture that emerges is one of greater disadvantage for women workers in general and those belonging to rural as well as SCs/STs in particular. Apart from such inherited disadvantages as lower social position, a number of other factors also contribute to such a picture. These are their limited asset position, access to resources, and low level of education and skill. Education, and consequently some ability to acquire formal skills, could be a moderating force but this aspect presents a dismal picture. The overall situation of women workers calls for interventions of a promotional nature from different entry points but with a strong emphasis on education.

In spite of promises and commitments and focus on women's development and empowerment, the present status of women continues to be quite dismal in terms of important human development parameters like health, nutrition, literacy, educational attainments, skill levels, occupational status etc. There are a number of gender-specific barriers which prevent women for gaining access to their rightful share in the flow of public goods and services. Unless the felt needs of women are incorporated and mainstreamed in the planning and development process it is apprehended that the fruits of economic growth are likely to completely bypass a significant section of the country's population which does not augur well for the future growth of the economy. This calls for a focused priority the strengthening, expansion and universalisation of gender budgeting in all its aspects.

Improving the status and treatment of women is a major development challenge.

8

Social Empowerment of Women

Women and girls in India face a crisis of growing health needs. From the moment of conception to the end of life, the challenges to the female sex are enormous, especially those who are poor; suffer from multiple exclusions, including caste, class, geographic isolation and tribal status. Health policies have few specific strategies for improving access to marginalized groups.

8.1 Health Problems and Needs of Women

Discrimination against women and girls impinges upon their right to health and manifests itself in the form of worsening health and nutrition indices. Thus, India continues to grapple with unacceptably high maternal mortality rate (MMR), infant mortality rate (IMR) and increasing rates of anaemia, malnutrition, HIV/AIDS among women.

Women also disproportionately lack access to health services. Inaccessibility of health centres and poverty prevent them from getting timely medical aid. Absence of toilets and drinking water adversely impacts their health.

Inadequacies of clean cooking fuels adversely impacts women and children's work burden, health and nutrition.

Women and girls spend a great deal of time gathering fuel, adversely affecting their productivity and education. Use of firewood and inferior fuels such as weeds or crop wastes leads to smoke-related ailments including respiratory diseases, cancer and cataracts resulting in blindness.

Malnutrition begins during infancy and sets in motion a life long cycle of poor health. Over half of all Indian women suffer from anaemia, which acerbates maternal morbidity. More women die of maternal death related causes in India than in any other country in the world. Women as a whole are especially susceptible to many diseases because of their poor nutritional standards and discriminatory practices in health inputs right from their birth.

Furthermore, every form of violence against women has steadily increased including rapes, dowry murder and domestic violence. Despite the alarming health crisis of women and girls, the national policy focus prioritizes family planning and reproductive health without addressing underlying issues such as women's low participation in decision-making, which adversely affects their health status. It is noteworthy that the leading killer of women in India is tuberculosis. Yet due to the focus on maternal and reproductive health this fact is little known and there are no gender-specific policies or programmes in place with regard to this disease.

8.1.1 HIV/AIDS: HIV in India is spreading from high-risk groups to the general population in many areas, and from urban to rural areas. Women are increasingly becoming the face of the HIV epidemic and there are biological, social, legal, cultural, political and economic factors that make them more vulnerable to HIV/AIDS. These factors, in turn, have an impact on women's access to services, resources, and information. Women have limited ability to negotiate safer sex and the risk and reality of sexual violence also means an increased risk of HIV transmission through unprotected non-consensual sex. In India, testing for the HIV virus is rare until symptoms set in. The numbers suffering from HIV/AIDS are therefore likely to be far higher than estimated. Once HIV/AIDS enters the home, family budgets are reversed forever because of loss of income earning opportunities and expenditure on medical care. Women are the major caregivers in most cases.

A multi-sectoral, decentralized, gender-sensitive and community-based health policy is needed. Effective strategies that address the relationships between gender and HIV/AIDS require a focus on gender within health care in general. There is perhaps an urgent need that the response to the HIV/AIDS epidemic be made multi-sectoral and be integrated into comprehensive, decentralized, participatory community-based health services. A focus on increasing women's ability to access preventive and treatment and care services is crucial.

8.1.2 Reproductive Health: The human rights of women include their right to have control over and decide freely and responsibly on matters related to their sexuality, including sexual and reproductive health, free of coercion, discrimination and violence. Equal relationships between women and men in matters of sexual relations and reproduction—including full respect for the integrity of the person—require mutual respect, consent and shared responsibility for sexual behaviour and its consequences.

Reproductive health is a state of complete physical, mental and social well-being—and not merely the absence of disease or infirmity—in all matters relating to the reproductive system and to its functions and processes. Reproductive health therefore implies that people are able to have a satisfying and safe sex life and that they have the capability to reproduce and the freedom to decide if, when and how often to do so. Implicit in this last condition is the right of men and women to be informed and to have access to safe, effective, affordable and acceptable methods of family planning of their choice, as well as other methods of their choice. In line with the above definition of reproductive health, reproductive health care is defined as the constellation of methods, techniques and services that contribute to reproductive health and well-being by preventing and solving reproductive health problems. It also includes sexual health, the purpose of which is the enhancement of life and personal relations, and not merely counselling and care related to reproduction and sexually transmitted diseases.

Bearing in mind the above definition, reproductive rights embrace certain human rights that are already recognized in national laws, international human rights documents and other consensus documents. These rights rest on the recognition of the basic right of all couples and individuals to decide freely and responsibly the number, spacing and timing of their children and to have the information and means to do so, and the right to attain the highest standard of sexual and reproductive health. It also includes their right to make decisions concerning reproduction free of discrimination, coercion and violence, as expressed in human rights documents. In the exercise of this right, they should take into account the needs of their living and future children and their responsibilities towards the community. The promotion of the responsible exercise of these rights for all people should be the fundamental basis for government- and community-supported policies and programmes in the area of reproductive health, including family planning.

Reproductive health eludes many of the world's women because of: (a) inadequate levels of knowledge about human sexuality and poor-quality reproductive health information and services, (b) prevalence of high-risk sexual behaviour (c) discriminatory social practices, (d) negative attitudes towards women and girls and (e) limited power many women and girls have over their sexual and reproductive lives. Adolescents are particularly vulnerable because of their lack of information and access to relevant services in most countries. Older women and men have distinct reproductive and sexual health issues which are often inadequately addressed.

8.1.3 Changing Pattern of Lifestyle Illness: India has made rapid strides in the health sector since Independence. With increased coverage and better access to health facilities, life expectancy in India has risen over the past 70 years. As per Census of India, in 2011-2015, the life expectancy for women stood at 70.0. As the life span increases, the incidence of chronic diseases is set to overtake infectious diseases. As many studies have pointed out, there are signs that India is entering the epidemiological transition with a change in disease patterns from infectious to chronic, degenerative and non-communicable diseases. This is attributed to improved nutrition, immunisation, and improved access to primary health care. In urban areas, more women are succumbing to newer lifestyle-related illnesses like diabetes, hypertension, cardiovascular and cancer.

A related issue is the fact that women in urban areas are often confined to the house and participate in the economy as home-based workers. To improve their conditions, more visibility is needed on the nature of the work and production system and the implications these might have for appropriate interventions.

8.1.4 Women and Ageing: Demographic ageing is a global phenomenon. With a comparatively young population, India is still poised to become home to the second largest number of older persons in the world. The asymmetry in the population pyramid with males outnumbering females as a whole and females outnumbering males at the upper end of the age spectrum is a peculiar feature of the Indian population.

There is lack of disaggregated data to assess the number of services availed of by aged women and their impact. The Government has committed itself to providing social security for the aged woman. The discrimination and subordination that the old women suffer, the glaring difference in education and literacy, income differentials between men and women are being looked into by Government for state intervention.

8.1.5 Specific Micronutrient Deficiencies in India: Some of the specific micronutrient deficiencies in the country which are of a magnitude that causes public health concerns are described below.

A. Iron Deficiency Anaemia (IDA): IDA is the most widespread micronutrient deficiency in the world affecting more than a billion people. It affects all age groups irrespective of gender, race, caste, creed and religion with higher incidence among vulnerable groups in developing world. Anaemia is associated with increased susceptibility to infections, reduction in work capacity and poor concentration. In India, this silent emergency is rampant among women belonging to reproductive age group, children and low socio-economic strata of the population. IDA reduces the capacity to learn and work, resulting in lower productivity and loss of wages, limiting economic and social development. Anaemia in pregnant women leads to adverse pregnancy outcomes such as high maternal and neonatal mortality, low birth weight, increased risk of obstetrical complications, increased morbidity and serious impairment of the physical and mental development of the child. Anaemia remains one of the major indirect causes of maternal mortality in India. In children, anaemia causes low scholastic skills leading many of them to be below average in classes or premature dropping out from schools. It also triggers increased morbidity from infectious diseases.

It is also seen that children born to mothers who were illiterate or who belonged to scheduled castes/tribes were more likely to be anaemic than their counterparts. Further, children born to moderately and severely anaemic mothers were also anaemic, reflecting the consequences of poor maternal health status on the health of the children. Research studies have suggested that severe iron deficiency anaemia during the first two years of life, when the brain is still developing, may cause permanent neurological damage adding further sense of urgency to the current efforts to prevent iron deficiency anaemia in children.

The current strategy, included as part of Reproductive and Child Health Programme (RCH) under National Rural Health Mission, recommends that pregnant and lactating women, infants, school children and adolescents should be targeted in the Nutritional Anaemia Prophylaxis Programme as per the recommended dosage.

B. Iodine Deficiency Disorders (IDDs): IDDs are a major public health problem for populations throughout the world, particularly for pregnant women and young children. They are a threat to the social and economic development of countries. The most devastating outcomes of iodine deficiency are increased pre-natal mortality and mental retardation. Iodine deficiency is the greatest cause of preventable brain damage in childhood which is the primary motivation behind the current worldwide drive to eliminate it. The main factor responsible for iodine deficiency is a low dietary supply of iodine. It occurs in populations living in areas where the soil has low iodine content as a result of past glaciations or the repeated leaching effects of snow, water and heavy rainfall. Crops grown in this soil, therefore, do not provide adequate amounts of iodine when consumed.

Goitre is the most visible manifestation of IDDs. In severely endemic areas, cretinism may affect up to 5-15 percent of the population. While cretinism is the most extreme manifestation, of considerably greater significance are the more subtle degrees of mental impairment leading to poor school performance, reduced intellectual ability and impaired work capacity.

IDDs have been recognized as a public health problem in India since the 1920s. No State in India is completely free from IDDs. A third of all children in the world that are born with IDD-related mental damage live in India.

Indian National Goitre Control Programme (NGCP) was started in 1962 with a focus on the goitre belt in the country. However, the programme of universal iodization was introduced only in 1984, when all edible salt in the market was required to offer 30 ppm (parts per million) iodine at the production level. This was legalized through the PFA (Prevention of Food Adulteration) Act, 1988 that also banned the availability of crystalline salt (non-iodized) as an edible product. It was accepted variably by the different States, some putting only a partial ban and others none at all.

Based on the recommendations of the Central Council of Health, the Government took a policy decision to iodise the entire edible salt in the country by 1992. Since 1992, the National Iodine Deficiency Disorders Control Programme (NIDDCP) is the new name given to the erstwhile National Goitre Control Programme. This change has been effected with a view to cover the wide spectrum of iodine deficiency, such as mental and physical retardation, deaf-mutism and cretinism, under the programme. Due to various research reports, the Central Government lifted the ban on the sale of non-iodized salt in 2000. The States chose to retain or revoke the ban depending upon their own assessment. In 2005, a country-wide universal ban on sale of non-iodized salt for human consumption was again been promulgated by the Central Government.

C. Vitamin A Deficiency (VAD): Vitamin A is an important micronutrient for maintaining normal growth, regulating cellular proliferation and differentiation, controlling development, and maintaining visual and reproductive functions. Vitamin A deficiency is one of the major deficiencies among lower income strata population in India. Human beings cannot produce this micronutrient in the body itself. Hence, it has to be externally provided. This deficiency is seen greater in pre-school children and pregnant and lactating women due to higher need for this micronutrient. In severe cases it can even lead to total blindness.

VAD has been recognized as a major controllable public health and nutritional problem. An estimated 5.7 percent children in India suffer from eye signs of vitamin A deficiency. Recent evidence suggests that even mild vitamin A deficiency probably increases morbidity and mortality in children, emphasizing the public health importance of this disorder.

Way back in 1970, a National Programme for Prevention of Nutritional Blindness was initiated to fight this deficiency. The beneficiaries of this programme were pre-school children (1-5 years). Further, the programme was modified in 1992 to cover children in the age group of 9 months to 3 years only. Presently, Vitamin A supplementation exists as an integral component of RCH programme which is a part of National Rural Health Mission. Ministry of Health and Family Welfare, Government of India, issued guidelines to the States in November 2006 extending the programme to cover children up to 5 years.

8.2 Nutrition Support

Although the country has been able to eliminate nutritional deficiency syndrome like pellagra, beriberi, scurvy etc. yet chronic energy deficiency among adults, under-nutrition among children and micronutrient deficiencies are still prevalent across all section of the population. The country has adopted a multi-sectoral and multi-pronged strategy to combat these problems and to improve the nutritional status of the population.

One half of the children under the age of 5 years in India are moderately or severely malnourished, 30 percent of newborn children are significantly under weight and nearly 60 percent of women are anaemic. Under the Integrated Child Development Scheme (ICDS), the Department of Women and Child Development implements the food supplementation programme for improving nutritional status of mothers and children. Ministry of Health and Family Welfare implements programmes for tackling major micronutrient deficiencies such as vitamin A and iodine deficiency etc.

To address the needs of under-nourished infants and children below 3 years, 15 percent of the total Additional Central Assistance (ACA) is earmarked for the nutrition component under the Pradhan Mantri Gramodaya Yojana (PMGY). ACA under the nutrition component of PMGY is an additionality for providing nutrition to children in 0-3 years. States are required to ensure that all below poverty line (BPL) children in 0-3 years are registered for PMGY and provided requisite nutrition.

The programme of Nutritional Support to Primary Education, popularly known as Mid-day Meal Scheme, was launched in 1995 as a fully-funded Centrally Sponsored Scheme. Under this scheme, all children in primary schools in government and government-aided schools are covered. Ideally, a hot meal is provided to the children at school for 10 months in a year. The foodgrains are delivered directly at the district level by the Food Corporation of India, under instructions from the Department of Education in the Government of India.

8.3 Women Education, Training and Skill Development

There is an increased awareness that education is one of the most valuable means of achieving gender equality and the empowerment of women. Education is seen as a critical factor in breaking the inter-generational cycle of transmission of poverty. The power of education lies not just in imparting formal literacy, but rather in the acquisition of skills that enable access to multiple literacy—economic, legal, health, political and media etc.

Education is a key intervention in initiating and sustaining processes of empowerment. Good quality education can help women and marginalized communities to: (a) improve their status, (b) enable them to have greater access to information and resources and (c) challenge various forms of discrimination. Education helps strengthen democratic processes as it allows for greater and more equitable participation. Being educated, leads to greater self-confidence and self-esteem. It enables engagement with development processes and institutions of governance from a position of strength. Poor women from socially disadvantaged communities are invariably not literate and therefore find themselves at a disadvantage when participating in development processes.

It is, however, important to recognise that while being literate or educated is necessary for empowerment, it does not automatically ensure it. For that a society needs an education system which is of good quality and promotes critical thinking. From the perspective of gender this means that education and literacy should enable women and girls to critically analyse their situations, raise questions about their subordination and help them make informed choices. It is well-known that the institution of schooling is an important site for socialisation that actually reinforces rather than challenges patriarchy and gender discrimination. It is in this context that the content and pedagogy of education become critical.

The focus of educational planning is generally on formal education but this is only one dimension of the educational provisioning, especially when needs of deprived women are under consideration and empowerment of women is the main objective.

8.3.1 Sexual Harassment, Violence and Women Education: Sexual harassment and violence against girls and young women within educational institutions is widespread but under-reported. There are systematic mechanisms to gather data that indicate the extent of the problem. While some universities have formulated guidelines and established mechanisms to deal with sexual harassment, many educational institutions still do not have policies. Though technically the guidelines should cover schools, no efforts have been made to implement the guidelines in schools where sexual harassment is fairly common but is rarely reported. One only has the media (print and electronic) to rely on for such information. Another area that has not received much attention is the impact of conflict and communal and sectarian violence on education. Communal and sectarian violence and long-term conflicts severely impact opportunities for girls and women's education. In volatile situations girls are kept away from schools.

In parts of India, like the North East and Kashmir, that have been experiencing conflict for several years, the ground level situation reveals that prolonged violence has negatively impacted the education systems there and the education opportunities for women and girls in various ways. Dropout rate of girls is high because of fear, insecurity, restricted mobility, displacement, migration etc. School participation and quality of education for girls is impacted by measures to control women's sexuality and mobility, like diktats imposing a dress code by religious bodies, militants or separatist groups.

In such situations schooling and other educational interventions can bring about a semblance of normalcy and prevent alienation from the mainstream. No systematic efforts have been made to understand and monitor the impact of conflict on education, especially women and girls. There are no policy guidelines on how to respond to the impact of violence and conflict. There are no mandated special provisions to deal with the particular problems arising out of such situations. Education provisioning, from gender perspective, should find a place in any policy on internal displacements and associated relief and rehabilitation measures.

8.4 Beti Bachao Campaign

It is a campaign in India to end the gender selective abortion of female foetuses, which skewed the population towards a significant under representation of girls in some Indian states. The *Beti Bachao* campaign is supported by human rights group, non-governmental organisations, and the state and local governments in India.

Beti Bachao activities include large rallies, poster campaigns, wall paintings, bill boards, and television commercials and short animations and video films. Celebrities such as video director—Jagmeet Bal and bollywood actress Priyanka Chopra, have become involved in Save the Girl Child initiatives.

The Beti Bachao campaign is supported by numerous medical organisations in India, including the Indian Medical Association.

Government support at the state level has provided funding for Beti Bachao publicity activities in particular. The expenditures related to the campaign have been a source of political controversy in Madhya Pradesh, which launched its official Beti Bachao Abhiyan campaign in 2012.

The campaign has reported some success in parts of India. In 2009, it was reported that in Gujarat, rate of female births increased from 802 to 882 for every 1,000 male births. Beti Bachao activities were credited with this improvement.

Apart from the programmes mentioned above, the Government of Himachal Pradesh launched a scheme named Beti Hai Anmol and for below poverty line families to incentivize the birth of girl child up to two children and encourage families to place scholarship up to 12th standard through conditional cash transfer. As per the state's latest evaluation on sex ratio, the state has improved from 904 females for 1,000 males in 2008 to 922. Uttarakhand state has also given a fixed deposit amount of ₹ 5,000 to a newborn girl child from BPL families under the *Nandadevi Kanya Scheme* to stop female foeticide in the state.

8.5 Beti Bachao Beti Padhao (BBBP)

On January 22, 2015, Prime Minister Shri Narendra Modi launched the *Beti Bachao, Beti Padhao* campaign from Panipat in Haryana. The campaign is aimed at increasing the low value that Indian society puts on the girl child.

The Census (2011) data showed a significant declining trend in the Child Sex Ratio (CSR), calculated as number of girls for every 1,000 boys between age group of 0-6 years, with an all time low of 918 in 2011 from 976 in 1961. The decline in CSR has been unabated since 1961. This is an alarming indicator for women disempowerment. It reflects both, pre-birth discrimination manifested through gender biased sex selection, and post-birth discrimination against girls. The decline is widespread across the country and has expanded to rural as well as tribal areas.

Alarmed by the sharp decline, the Government of India has introduced Beti Bachao, Beti Padhao (BBBP) programme to address the issue of decline in CSR in 100 gender critical districts. Co-ordinated and convergent efforts are needed to ensure survival, protection and education of the girl child.

8.5.1 Objectives of BBBP: The overall goal of BBBP Scheme is to celebrate the girl child and enable her education. The objectives of the scheme are as under:

1. Prevent gender biased sex selective elimination.
2. Ensure survival and protection of the girl child.
3. Ensure education of the girl child.

8.5.2 Components of BBBP: BBBP initiative has two major components.

1. **Mass Communication Campaign:** The campaign aims at ensuring girls are born, nurtured and educated without discrimination to become empowered citizens of this country. The campaign interlinks National, State and district level interventions with community level action in 100 districts, bringing together different stakeholders for accelerated impact.
2. **Multi-sectoral Interventions in 100 Gender Critical Districts Covering all States/UTs:** Co-ordinated and convergent efforts are undertaken in close co-ordination with MoHFW and MoHRD to ensure survival, protection and education of the girl child. The district collectors or deputy commissioners (DCs) lead and co-ordinate actions of all departments for implementation of BBBP at the district level. Mulit-sectoral interventions include the following:

- **Ministry of WCD:** Promote registration of pregnancies in first trimester in Anganwadi Centres (AWCs); undertake training of stakeholders; community mobilization and sensitization; involvement of gender champions; reward and recognition of institutions and frontline workers.
- **Ministry of Health and Family Welfare:** Monitor implementation of Pre-Conception and Pre-Natal Diagnostic Techniques (PCP&DT) Act, 1994; increased institutional deliveries; registration of births; strengthening PNDT cells; setting up monitoring committees.
- **Ministry of Human Resource Development:** Universal enrolment of girls; decreased drop-out rate; girl child friendly standards in schools; strict implementation of Right to Education (RTE); construction of functional toilets for girls.

8.6 One Stop Centre Scheme

Gender-based violence (GBV) is a global health, human

rights and development issue that transcends geography, class, culture, age, race and religion to affect every community and country in every corner of the world. Article 1 of UN Declaration on the Elimination of Violence, 1993, provides a definition of gender-based abuse, calling it "any act of gender-based violence that results in, or is likely to result in, physical, sexual or psychological harm or suffering to women, including threats of such acts, coercion or arbitrary deprivation of liberty, whether occurring in public or in private life".

In India, gender-based violence has many manifestations; from the more universally prevalent forms of domestic and sexual violence including rape, to harmful practices such as, dowry, honour killings, acid attacks, witch-hunting, sexual harassment, child sexual abuse, trafficking for commercial sexual exploitation, child marriage, sex selective abortion, sati etc. Other than these, India is also grappling with violence due to inequities in social life more particularly in times of displacement and communal incidents.

8.6.1 Background: The Twelfth Plan Working Group on Women's Agency and Empowerment had recommended setting up of one stop crisis centres, on pilot basis, for providing shelter, police desk, legal, medical and counselling services to victims of violence under one roof integrated with a 24 hour helpline.

Justice (Retd.) Usha Mehra Commission, set up to suggest measures to improve women's safety had recommended in its report submitted on February 22, 2013, that there is need for establishment of a "one-stop centre" at a notified hospital to help victims of sexual assault and ensure speedy punishment to culprits.

Ministry of Finance, Government of India has established Nirbhaya Fund with an initial corpus of ₹ 1,000 crore (as per the announcement in Budget 2013-14) for women safety pertaining to the strategic areas of prevention, protection and rehabilitation. For subsequent financial years of 2014-15 and 2015-16, an amount of ₹ 1,000 crore (each financial year) was provided under the Nirbhaya Fund.

In light of the above, Ministry of Women and Child Development (MWCD), has formulated a Centrally-sponsored Scheme for setting up One Stop Centre, a sub-scheme of Umbrella Scheme for National Mission for Empowerment of women including *Indira Gandhi Mattritav Sahyaog Yojana*. These Centres will be established across the country to provide integrated support and assistance under one roof to women affected by violence, both in private and public spaces in phased manner. In the first phase, one centre shall be established in every State/UT on a pilot basis.

8.6.2 Location: For establishing a centre, the first preference would be to obtain suitable and adequate accommodation having carpet area of at least 132 square metres within a hospital/medical facility. If it is not possible to locate accommodation within a hospital or medical facility, then an existing government/semi-government institutions located within 2 kilometre radius of the hospital/medical facility in the district headquarter having adequate accommodation will be used for operating the centre.

If it is not possible to locate the centre in the existing accommodation, the centre could be constructed on adequate land either within hospital/medical facility or within 2 kilometre radius of the hospital/medical facility. The requirement for construction of building of centres will be assessed, after taking into account of non-availability of existing accommodation. The centres could be constructed on the adequate and suitable land having at least total area of 300 square metres identified by State Government, if required. A provision of ₹ 7.54 crore was kept for construction of 20 centres.

8.6.3 Services: The One Stop Centre will provide support and assistance to women affected by violence, both in private and public spaces. In case girls under 18 years of age are referred to the centre, they will also be served in co-ordination with authorities/institutions established under the Juvenile Justice (Care and Protection of Children) Act, 2000 and Protection of Children from Sexual Offence Act, 2012. The centres will be integrated with a women helpline to provide a range of services

8.7 Universalisation of Women Helpline (WHL) Scheme, 2016

The scheme of Universalisation of Women Helpline is intended to provide 24 hours immediate and emergency response to women affected by violence through referral (linking with appropriate authority such as police, One Stop Centre, hospital) and information about women related government schemes programmes across the country through a single uniform number.

Women helpline (WHL) will be integrated with One Stop Centre Scheme (OSC) under which one OSC shall be established in every State/UT to provide integrated support and assistance to women affected by violence, both in private and public spaces under one roof. Women affected by violence and in need of redressal services will be referred to OSC through WHL.

Under the WHL scheme, the States/UTs will utilise or augment their existing women helplines through a dedicated single national number. Department of Telecommunication, Government of India has allocated short code 181 to all States/UTs which is being used by some States/UTs such as Delhi, Chandigarh, Chhattisgarh as women helpline. Under this Scheme, States/UTs need to adopt this short code 181 as women helpline (WHL). It is envisaged that this number would be compatible with all the existing telecommunication channels whether providing post/pre-paid mobile or landline services through any public or private network. All the state/district/city level helplines, whether private or public, would be integrated with this women helpline.

The objectives of the scheme are as under:

- To provide toll-free 24 hours telecom service to women affected by violence, seeking support and information.
- To facilitate crisis and non-crisis intervention through referral to the appropriate agencies such as

police/hospitals/ambulance services/district legal service authority (DLSA)/protection officer (PO)/OSC.

- To provide information about the appropriate support services, government schemes and programmes available to woman affected by violence, in her particular situation within the local area in which she resides or is employed.

The scheme covers any woman or girl facing violence within public or private sphere of life or seeking information about women related programmes or schemes.

WHL will be universalised through short code 181 number by augmenting/using the infrastructure of existing helplines working at the State/UT level. States/UTs will have the option of locating the helpline centre in capital or in any other city as per their requirement. However, while selecting the location of the WHL, due care needs to be taken by the States/UTs for its integration with the OSC.

8.8 Ujjawala

Effective April 1, 2016, it is a comprehensive scheme for prevention of trafficking and rescue, rehabilitation and re-integration of victims of trafficking for commercial sexual exploitation.

8.8.1 Background: Trafficking of women and children for commercial sexual exploitation is an organized crime that violates basic human rights. India has emerged as a source, destination and transit for both in-country and cross-border trafficking. The problem of trafficking of women and children for commercial sexual exploitation is especially challenging due to its myriad complexities and variation. Poverty, low status of women, lack of a protective environment etc. are some of the causes for trafficking.

A multi-sectoral approach is needed which will undertake preventive measures to arrest trafficking especially in vulnerable areas and sections of population; and to enable rescue, rehabilitation and reintegration of the trafficked victims.

Keeping the above issues and gaps in mind the Ministry of Women and Child Development, Government of India formulated this scheme called *Ujjawala*. The scheme has been conceived primarily for the purpose of preventing trafficking on the one hand and rescue and rehabilitation of victims on the other.

8.8.2 Objective of the Scheme: These are as under:

To prevent trafficking of women and children for commercial sexual exploitation through social mobilization and involvement of local communities, awareness generation programmes, public discourses through workshops/seminars and such events and any other innovative activity.

1. To facilitate rescue of victims from the place of their exploitation and place them in safe custody.
2. To provide rehabilitation services both immediate and long-term to the victims by providing basic amenities such as shelter, food, clothing, medical treatment including counselling, legal aid and guidance and vocational training.
3. To facilitate reintegration of the victims into the family and society at large.
4. To facilitate repatriation of cross-border victims to their country of origin.

8.8.3 Target Group/Beneficiaries:

- Women and children who are vulnerable to trafficking for commercial sexual exploitation.
- Women and children who are victims of trafficking for commercial sexual exploitation.

8.9 Nari Shakti Puruskar

Every year, Ministry of Women and Child Development celebrates International Women Day on March 8. The significance of the International Women's Day lies in re-affirmation of society's commitment to improve the conditions of women, especially those at the margins and empower them to take rightful place in society.

Nari Shakti Puruskars are conferred every year. The

awards are conferred on March 8 on the occasion of International Women's Day (IWD). The award in each category carries a certificate and a cash amount. The award is given to eminent or outstanding institutions or organizations and individuals. With the institution of these awards all the earlier women awards given by the Ministry of Women and Child Development ceased to exist.

The awards are given in the following categories:

1. Rani Rudramma Devi Award for best panchayat/village community.
2. Mata Jijabai Award for best urban local body for providing services and facilities to women.
3. Kannagi Devi Award for best state which has appreciably improved child sex ratio.
4. Rani Gaidinliu Zeliang Award for best civil society organization (CSO) doing outstanding work for the welfare and well-being of women.
5. Devi Ahilyabai Holkar Award for best private sector organization/public sector undertaking in promoting the well-being and welfare of women.
6. Rani Lakshmibai Award for best institution for research and development in the field of women empowerment.
7. Award for courage and bravery.
8. Awards for making outstanding contributions to women's endeavour, community work, making a difference and women empowerment.

8.10 Mahila Police Volunteers (MPVs)

Gender-based violence (GBV) faced by women both in public and private spaces, including domestic violence, sexual assault, rape, voyeurism, stalking etc. are a major threat to women equality and empowerment. A gender responsive police service requires specific training, increased presence of female personnel within the police force and community outreach to integrate gender issues into policies, protocols and operational procedures.

In recent years, there has been enactment of various legislations by the Parliament which address the issue of GBV, i.e. the Criminal Law Amendment Act, 2013; Sexual Harassment of Women at Workplace (Prevention, Prohibition and Redressal) Act, 2013; and Protection of Women from Domestic Violence Act, 2005

Role of police is pivotal in safety and security of citizens in general and women in particular. To increase the visibility of women in the police force, Home Ministry has carried forward the initiative to give 33 percent reservation to women in police force by implementing it in UTs and propagating in the States. There has been an increasing emphasis on gender sensitivity of police force through training programmes, performance appraisal, women police stations to tackle crime against women. An advisory dated May 12, 2015 by the Home Ministry stressed on the need for sensitivity in handling women's issues.

However, it is a matter of common knowledge that women who are victim of violence or harassment may not find it easy to approach the police or other authorities for getting help or support. It would, therefore, be desirable to provide them an effective alternative for getting help and support.

In order to promote these objectives and increase focused community outreach, Government of India envisages engagement and nomination of Mahila Police Volunteers (MPVs) in all States and UTs who will act as a link between police and community and facilitate women in distress. This will be done in a phased manner.

MPVs are envisaged as empowered, responsible, socially aware women for fostering leadership in local settings to facilitate police outreach on gender concerns. They will be an interface between the society and police.

An MPV will serve as a public-police interface in order to fight crime against women. The broad mandate of MPVs is to report incidences of violence against women such as domestic violence, child marriage, dowry harassment and violence faced by women in public spaces. She will act as a role model for the community.

An MPV is an honorary position. The Scheme in the first phase will be implemented on pilot basis in all States and UTs. In the first phase, two districts from every state and one district from every UT shall be chosen on the basis of the following criteria: (a) child sex ratio and (b) crime against women

The final selection of the district/districts would be the responsibility of the concerned State/UT.

An MPV could be any woman who is socially and voluntarily committed towards empowerment of women and girls, willing to raise her voice against gender-based violence and support the police in creating a gender just society free from violence. The MPVs will be chosen by the Home Department of the concerned State/UT through the Superintendent of Police of the district. The MPV will directly report to the Circle Inspector in the Police Thana. A woman nominated as an MPV shall be entrusted with the task of acting as a link between the police and the society on gender concerns. MPVs will as act as a facilitating link between the citizens and the police.

9

Political Empowerment of Women

In the early years of the Independence of India in 1947, much of the country's governance was in the hands of elected representatives and the official machinery. Such a centralized approach did not produce desired results, especially in terms of the inclusion of marginalized groups within the governance processes. Constitutional, legislative and policy reforms since then and the continued administrative decentralization have increased the political participation of marginalized groups, especially poor women. Women's increased political participation has yielded positive results. Issues central to development—including health, nutrition, family income and education—have taken centre-stage as women participate in panchayati raj institutions (PRI), village development boards and other governance structures.

9.1 Need for Gender Balancing in Decision-making

There has been growing acceptance of the importance to society of the full participation of women in decision-making and power at all levels and in all fora, including inter-governmental, governmental, and non-governmental sectors. In some countries, women have also attained higher positions in these spheres. An increasing number of countries applied affirmative and positive action policies, including quota systems or voluntary agreements in some countries, measurable goals and targets, developed training programmes for women's leadership and introduced measures to reconcile family and work responsibilities of both women and men. National mechanisms and machineries for the advancement of women as well as national and international networks of women politicians, parliamentarians, activists and professionals in various fields have been established or upgraded and strengthened.

Despite general acceptance of the need for a gender balance in decision-making bodies at all levels, a gap between *de jure* and *de facto* equality has persisted. Notwithstanding substantial improvements of *de jure* equality between women and men, the actual participation of women at the highest levels of national and international decision-making has not significantly changed and gross under-representation of women in decision-making bodies in all areas, including *inter alia* politics, conflict prevention and resolution mechanisms, the economy, the environment and the media hinders the inclusion of a gender perspective in these critical spheres of influence. Women continue to be underrepresented at the legislative, ministerial and sub-ministerial levels, as well as at the highest levels of the corporate sector and other social and economic institutions.

Traditionally assigned gender roles limit women's choices in education and careers and compel women to assume the burden for household responsibilities.

Initiatives and programmes aimed at women's increased participation in decision-making are hindered by a host of factors, among which the following are prominent:

1. Lack of human and financial resources for training and advocacy for political careers.
2. Gender-sensitive attitudes towards women in society.
3. Lack of accountability of elected officials and political parties for promoting gender equality and women's participation in public life.
4. Lack of social awareness of the importance of balanced participation of women and men in decision-making.
5. Lack of willingness on the part of men to share power; sufficient dialogue and co-operation with women's non-governmental organizations, along with organizational and political structures, which enable all women to participate in all spheres of political decision-making.

9.2 Gender Inclusion in Legislatures, Judiciary and Police

While the planning process and public expenditure in terms of programmes and schemes are sought to be included in gender budgeting, yet without gender sensitivity of important organs such as police and judiciary, the implementation will not be successful. This is especially true of schemes which have a strong element of protection or are rights based. For example, if a woman is not given her due share of property or other assets as per law, it is essential that these agencies help and support her in getting her share without much delay or harassment. This can happen only if gender sensitivity is inculcated in such bodies and they are made aware of the laws, policies, programmes and other initiatives for women. It is also important that justice delivery is quick with the enforcement machinery being responsive and gender sensitive to women's needs especially in cases of domestic violence and personal assault.

It is, therefore, necessary to induct a larger number of women in these bodies at different levels. This will encourage women to actively participate in power sharing and active participation in decision-making. Efforts should be made to provide coaching facilities and support services so that women can compete along with men both at entry and to facilitate upward mobility of women in these institutions.

The setting up of women police stations, women's help desk in every police station, and increasing the strength of women police to 30 percent of the total force has been reiterated a number of times by the Ministry of Women and Child Development in a number of forums. The Ministry of Home Affairs should take requisite steps to fulfil their obligations towards gender budgeting by engendering the police force.

True, efforts have been made to empower women socially, economically and politically, but as a result of the lack of synergy or coordination between these activities, the outcomes are not satisfactory. For example, the increasing induction of women representatives into the PRIs should have meant automatic improvement in the lives of rural women, but if it has not happened, it is because the elected women were not educated or literate or even made aware of their rights. Also there are many groups of women who on account of tradition, culture, ethnic, social or religious background are more vulnerable compared to the women in the mainstream sector.

It is imperative that an integrated policy and strategy be formulated that addresses economic, social, and political empowerment simultaneously and holistically along with the requisite programmes and schemes. Once such a comprehensive policy and programs flowing from it are put in place, it will be possible to enable an all round development of women, which will usher in true empowerment.

To sum up, notable constitutional, legislative and policy reforms, and continued administrative decentralization have demonstrated the commitment of Governments (Centre and States) to increase political participation of women at grassroots level. Although only one-third of seats were reserved for women by the Seventy-third and Seventy-fourth Constitutional Amendments, the actual representation is higher at all levels. Increased political participation of women has yielded a range of positive results, not only for women but also for their families and communities. Central issues in development such as health, nutrition, family income and education are finding their way to the top of the agenda for action. Women's participation brings about more inclusive governance and effective community-cantered development. Yet in many places, especially in states like UP, Bihar and Rajasthan, women continue to serve as proxies.

Over the years, efforts towards gender sensitisation of a traditionally male-dominated society have been intensified. These have included the following: (a) gender sensitisation of the law enforcement agencies—especially the police and the judiciary—through periodic training given by Government agencies and NGOs, (b) gender sensitisation of the training given by the National Judicial Academy, (c) gender sensitisation module of State level training institutions for the orientation of officials, (d) sensitisation of medical officers who are responsible for implementing the Prenatal Diagnostic Techniques (Prevention of Misuse and Regulation) Act and (e) National Research and Training Centre set up at the country's premier institution, the Lal Bahadur Shastri National Academy of Administration, for the training of administrators seeks to impart training in gender concerns.

9.3 Women in Local Bodies

Towns and cities contribute substantially to the economic development of the country. These urban centres also play an important support role in the development of rural hinterland. To keep this economic transformation in line with needs and realities at the grassroots level, it is necessary that the people and their representatives are fully involved in the planning and implementation of the programmes at local level. If democracy in Parliament and State Legislatures is to remain strong and stable, its roots must reach towns and villages and the cities where the people live.

9.3.1 Decentralisation Initiative, 1992 and Reservation of Seats for Women: The Seventy-third and Seventy-fourth Amendment Bills relating to *panchayats* and municipalities respectively were introduced in the Parliament in September 1991 to provide constitutional remedy for the inadequacies plaguing these bodies which were unable to perform effectively as vibrant democratic units of self-government. The Bills were referred to two joint bodies of Parliament and after necessary revision were reintroduced in July 1992, and passed by Parliament in December 1992. Both the Bills were ratified by the required number of States [Article 368(ii)] and the President gave his assent in April 1993. The Seventy-third Amendment Act relating to *panchayats* came into force from April 24, 1993. The Seventy-fourth Amendment Act relating to municipalities came into force from June 1, 1993. The changes made by the Seventy-third and Seventy-fourth Amendment Acts to the Constitution were of historical importance.

In short, *panchayats* and municipalities are now constitutional bodies forming third tier to the federal polity of India. India's decentralisation initiative in the form of Seventy-third and Seventy-fourth Amendments poses challenges and offers opportunities.

Legislative enactments have dramatically increased women's access to decision-making structures in recent years. The Seventy-third and Seventy-fourth Constitutional Amendments passed in 1993 provide for reservation of 33 percent of elected seats for women at different levels of local governance in both rural and urban local bodies. Also there would be one-third reservation for women to posts of chairperson of these bodies. One-third of the seats are further reserved for women belonging to the SC/ST community. The Panchayats (Extension to Schedule Areas) Act 1996 (PESA) made this amendment applicable to Schedule V areas. This has dramatically increased women's participation in local bodies. For every 5 year tenure of local governments, about 1 million women get elected to panchayats and local bodies. In some states, the number of elected women exceeds the reserved one-third quota.

The Constitution provides for rotation of seats reserved for women but does not prescribe the number of terms for which seats may be served for rotation. Seats are reserved for one term, two terms or more depending upon the provisions made by the State Legislature in the State law. The option to reserve seats for more than one terms is open, but it is for the State Legislature to decide the number of terms for which seats will remain reserved. Tamil Nadu has taken a positive step by freezing the reserved seats for women for two terms.

Local government institutions have not been given full financial and political powers to function independently but 29 subjects ranging from agriculture to poverty eradication have been devolved to these institutions. In theory, the presidents of the gram panchayats, block panchayats and district panchayats are responsible for prioritising the developmental needs of the villagers and allocating the grants accordingly. In practice, the level of responsiveness and manner of functioning of the panchayats varies considerably across states. As far as women's participation is concerned, the legislative enactments have ensured that they are represented in all states.

9.3.2 Lack of Confidence: Many of the elected women entering the public arena for the first time lack confidence, feel isolated, and have no previous political experience. They need to develop their innate leadership skills. Studies conducted in different parts of the country show that 95 percent of the elected women representatives (EWRs) are first-timers in politics and join politics because that is what their male family/village members want. As first timers without previous exposure to politics, many of the elected women lack the capacity to function properly in the panchayats and municipalities, and consequently are not taken seriously by their colleagues. Sustained training and networking efforts are being undertaken both by government and non-government agencies to ensure that women's capacity to participate improves. With just a few years of experience, women have emerged as articulate, motivated leaders all over the country.

Gender budgeting involving grassroots elected women representatives is being used for advocacy in several places. Increased networking and formation of confederations of elected women representatives has helped to strengthen women's leadership. This approach has been especially successful in southern and western India. The formation of these networks promotes solidarity among the elected women representatives, otherwise divided by caste, religion and geographical boundaries. Thus, formation of these networks is the first step in the direction of empowering women. Their position as panchayat members adds to their ability to intervene and negotiate with the community. The presence of

EWRs in the dispute resolution process lends support and confidence to other women. The networks have also been able to promote capacity building.

9.3.3 Proxy Politics: Constitutional provisions apart, there are complaints from various parts of the country regarding effective participation of women in local governance structures. Proxy politics, power brokering and gender discrimination continue, and many women sarpanches have to face violence for challenging existing societal power centres. In other cases, women are in PRI only in name. In reality, it is the male family members who hold the power. In spite of the affirmative action in panchayati raj in favour of marginalized communities, exclusion of caste, poverty, tribal status, gender and caste sharply demarcate those who have political power from those who do not. Central and State Governments should not delay any further the devolution and decentralization of powers from higher bodies (Government of India or State Governments) to the panchayati raj structures. This devolution right now is lagging in almost all the States. The three Fs—funds, functions and functionaries—in most States are still in the same position prior to 1993. In the absence of this basic requirement, the Constitutional provisions are not only being violated, but there is lack of clarity at the field level which leads to dysfunctional situations.

India has primarily relied upon the method of reservation to ensure women's presence in decision-making bodies. This has increased *de jure*, but not necessarily *de facto*, participation. There is need to encourage women's participation in other kinds of groups and associations which contribute to an atmosphere of leadership by women, as well as supporting training and networking for elected women.

10

Women and Media

10.1 Role of the Media in Women Portrayal

The existing law on regulating content in the media is contained in different sources. Thus, Article 51A of the Constitution states that it shall be the duty of every citizen of India to renounce practices derogatory to the dignity of women. Similarly, Section 294 of the IPC provides for penalties for obscene acts or conduct. The Indecent Representation of Women (Prohibition) Act, 1986 prohibits indecent representation of women through advertisement or in publications, writings, paintings, figures or in any other manner. The Act was enacted in the year 1986 and since then the issue of what is *obscene* has been a subject of great debate. The Act itself mostly revolves around how the object will affect society and the public morality rather than how it offends women.

The Indian Information Technology Act, 2000 has declared online pornography a punishable offence.

The role of the media in portraying women and the female gender as a whole leaves much to be desired. Press and the print media are generally found to unduly sensationalize traumatic events such as rape etc thereby invading the privacy of the victim. Very few positive stories of girls/women are published who have stood up for their rights or are achievers. Similarly, the electronic media and films portray serial/films highly derogatory to women, glorifying subservience of the woman to her husband/in laws, celebrating the birth of the boy child and portraying the disappointments of the family at the birth of the girl child. Eve teasing/sexual harassment is often a *fun* item in Indian films. As a result the general populace is fed on a regular diet of stories/news that are highly gender abusive, thus reinforcing traditional views that the women are an inferior race and can be freely exploited.

The media has perforce to become gender sensitive and more responsible when portraying women and thus play a significant role in bringing about attitudinal changes in the society. A gender-friendly media policy needs to be formulated for this purpose.

Negative, violent and/or degrading images of women including pornography, stereotyped portrayals, have increased in different forms using new communication technologies in some instances, and bias against women remains in the media. Poverty, the lack of access and opportunities, illiteracy, lack of computer literacy and language barriers, prevent women from using the information and communication technologies, including the internet. Development of and access to internet infrastructure is limited especially in developing countries and particularly for women.

The lack of gender sensitivity in the media is evidenced by the failure to eliminate the gender-based stereotyping and the reinforcement of women's traditional role that can be found in public and private media. The continued projection of negative and degrading images of women in media communications is evident. The world- wide trend towards consumerism has created a climate in which advertisements and commercial messages often portray women primarily as consumers and target girls and women of all ages inappropriately. Advertisements of beauty products, magazines and beauty pageants mushrooming all over have led to the creation of an image of an *ideal woman*.

Media policy needs to be gender proactive. There is a need to encourage media to project positive images and balanced portrayal of women and girls to enable attitudinal changes. The media policy should also help in generating awareness on gender issues and concerns so that the process of societal reorientation towards creating a gender just society gets widely disseminated.

10.2 Sex in Advertising

Sex in advertising is the use of sexual or erotic imagery (also called sex appeal) in advertising to draw interest to and to help sell a particular product. A feature of sex in advertising is that the imagery used, such as that of a pretty woman, typically has no connection to the product being advertised. The purpose of the imagery is to attract the attention of the potential customer or user. The type of imagery that may be used is very broad, and would include nudity.

The use of sex in advertising can be highly overt or extremely subtle. It ranges from relatively explicit displays of sexual acts, to the use of basic cosmetics to enhance attractive features. Sex has been utilized in advertising since its beginning. The earliest forms are wood carvings and illustrations of attractive women (often unclothed from the waist up) adorned posters, signs, and ads for saloons, tonics, and tobacco. In several notable cases, sex in advertising has been claimed as the reason for increased consumer interest and sales. Sex in advertising builds on the premise that people are curious about sexuality and that experience in marketing has been that sexuality sells products.

From a marketing point of view, sexuality can have biological, emotional/physical or spiritual aspects. The biological aspect of sexuality refers to the reproductive mechanism as well as the basic biological drive that exists in all species, which is hormonally controlled. The emotional or physical aspect of sexuality refers to the bond that exists between individuals, and is expressed through profound feelings or physical manifestations of emotions of love, trust, and caring. There is also a spiritual aspect of sexuality of an individual or as a connection with others.

Advertisers may and do use the various aspects of sexuality in advertisements. When sexuality is used in advertising, certain values and attitudes towards sex are necessarily *sold* along with a product. In advertising terms, this is called *the concept.*

Over the recent past, the use of increasingly explicit sexual imagery in consumer-oriented print advertising has become almost commonplace. In recent years, ads for jeans, perfumes and many other products have featured provocative images that are designed to elicit sexual responses from as large a cross section of the population as possible. Increased tolerance, more tempered censorship, emancipatory developments and increasing buying power of previously neglected appreciative target groups in rich markets have led to a marked increase in the share of attractive flesh *on display*.

Use of sexual imagery in advertising has been criticized on various grounds. Religious conservatives often consider it obscene or immodest. Some feminists and masculists claim it reinforces sexism by objectifying the individual.

Many advertisements are cantered around women posing seductively. Women are featured to lure in customers through their sex appeal. These thin, beautiful women are portrayed purely as objects, intended to please those who find their images pleasurable. Advertisers take advantage of this pleasing image and associate it with their products. Many companies are sacrificing the dignity and self-worth of women for the success of their products. Not only does this type of media cause men to view women as soulless bodies, but it causes women, young and old, to set impossible standards for their body images.

In advertisements, men are represented as independent. They are shown in more occupations than women. Women are represented mainly as housewives and mothers. Men are more likely to be shown advertising cars or business products, while women advertise domestic products. Men are more likely to be shown outdoors or in business settings. Women are depicted in domestic settings. Men are more often portrayed as authorities. As far as ads go, with age men seem to gain wisdom and authority. On the other hand, women seem to disappear with age.

To sum up, media plays a critical role in changing gender stereotypes. The approach to media strategy in India has been to use it as an instrument of change and to control its possible misuse. Media is encouraged to develop a code of conduct, professional guidelines, other self-regulatory mechanisms to remove gender stereotypes and promote a balanced portrayal of women and men.

Appendix

National Policy for Empowerment of Women (NPEW), 2001

Progress towards gender equality and women's empowerment in India has been built upon strong commitments by the government and unflagging effort by the women's movement. India's commitment to gender equality is further evidenced by the fact that it is a signatory to Convention on the Elimination of All Forms of Discrimination against Women (CEDAW), which was ratified on June 25, 1993 (with one reservation and two declaratory statements). India is also a signatory to the Convention on the Rights of the Child. The first report to the UN Committee of Experts on the Rights of the Child was submitted in 2000 and the second report in 2004.

In pursuance of the avowed objective of empowering the *women* as agents of socio-economic change, the National Policy on Empowerment of Women was adopted in April 2001. Gender inequality arising out of social norms and cultural traditions has been addressed through a range of direct and indirect measures, and the aim of the NPEW has been to bring about social change—changes in attitudes towards women, and women's empowerment. The policy itself reflects the aspirations of women and the women's movement. The effort is to bring gender justice and make *de jure* equality into *de facto* equality. Several State Governments have also formulated a policy for women's empowerment.

On the basis of NPEW, the National Plan of Action is being implemented which includes the following strategies:

1. To create an enabling environment for women to exercise their rights both within and outside their homes.
2. To reserve one-third of seats for women in the Lok Sabha and State Legislative Assemblies.

3. To adopt a special strategy for Women Component Plan to ensure that at least 30 percent of funds and benefits flow to women from all development sectors.
4. To organize women in self-help groups as a mark of the beginning of empowering them.
5. To accord high priority and ensure easy access to maternal and child health services.
6. To initiate steps for eliminating gender bias in all educational programmes; further to institute plans for free education of girls up to college levels including professional levels.
7. To equip women with necessary skills in modern upcoming trades which would make them economically independent and self-reliant.
8. To increase women's access to credit through setting up of Development Bank for women entrepreneurs in small and tiny sectors.

Various aspects of NPEW are as under.

Introduction

The principle of gender equality is enshrined in the Indian Constitution in its Preamble, Fundamental Rights, Fundamental Duties and Directive Principles of State Policy. The Constitution not only grants equality to women, but also empowers the State to adopt measures of positive discrimination in favour of women. Since Independence in 1947, there has been a marked shift in the approach to issues related to welfare, development and empowerment of women. Within the framework of a democratic polity, India's laws, development policies, schemes/programmes under Five Year Plans have aimed at advancement of women in different spheres. In recent years, the empowerment of women has been recognized as the central issue in determining the status of women. The National Commission for Women was set up by an Act of Parliament in 1990 to safeguard the rights and legal entitlements of women. The 73rd and 74th Amendments to the Constitution of India provided for reservation of seats for women in panchayats and municipalities, laying a strong foundation for their participation in decision-making at the local levels.

India has also ratified various international conventions and human rights instruments committing to secure equal rights for women. Key among them is the ratification of the Convention on Elimination of All Forms of Discrimination against Women (CEDAW) in 1993.

The Mexico Plan of Action (1975), the Nairobi Forward Looking Strategies (1985), the Beijing Declaration as well as the Platform for Action (1995) and the Outcome Document—adopted by the General Assembly Session of the United Nations on Gender Equality and Development and Peace for the 21st Century—titled "Further Actions and Initiatives to Implement the Beijing Declaration and the Platform for Action" have been unreservedly endorsed by India for appropriate follow up.

Objectives of the Policy

National Policy for Empowerment of Women, 2001 was formulated for bringing about advancement, development and empowerment of women in all spheres of life through creation of a more responsive judicial and legal system sensitive to women and mainstreaming a gender perspective in the development process. The strengthening and formation of relevant institutional mechanisms and implementation of international obligations/commitments and co-operation at the international, regional and sub-regional level was another commitment.

The primary objective of NPEW was to bring about the advancement, development and empowerment of women. Specifically, the objectives of this Policy included the following:

1. Creating an environment through positive economic and social policies for full development of women to enable them to realize their full potential.
2. The *de-jure* and *de-facto* enjoyment of all human rights and fundamental freedom by women on equal basis with

men in all spheres—political, economic, social, cultural and civil.

3. Equal access to participation and decision-making of women in social, political and economic life of the nation.
4. Equal access to women to healthcare, quality education at all levels, career and vocational guidance, employment, equal remuneration, occupational health and safety, social security and public office etc.
5. Strengthening legal systems aimed at elimination of all forms of discrimination against women.
6. Changing societal attitudes and community practices by active participation and involvement of both men and women.
7. Mainstreaming a gender perspective in the development process.
8. Elimination of discrimination and all forms of violence against women and the girl child.
9. Building and strengthening partnerships with civil society, particularly women's organizations.

Various Elements of NPEW

Politico-legal Empowerment of Women:

Legal-Judicial System: Legal-judicial system would be made more responsive and gender sensitive to women's needs, especially in cases of domestic violence and personal assault. New laws would be enacted and existing laws reviewed to ensure that justice is quick and the punishment meted out to the culprits is commensurate with the severity of the offence.

At the initiative of and with the full participation of all stakeholders including community and religious leaders, NPEW would aim to encourage changes in personal laws such as those related to marriage, divorce, maintenance and guardianship so as to eliminate discrimination against women.

The evolution of property rights in a patriarchal system has contributed to the subordinate status of women. NPEW would aim to encourage changes in laws relating to ownership of property and inheritance by evolving consensus in order to make them gender just.

Decision-making: Women's equality in power sharing and active participation in decision making, including decision-making in political process at all levels would be ensured for the achievement of the goals of empowerment. All measures would be taken to guarantee women equal access to and full participation in decision-making bodies at every level, including the legislative, executive, judicial, corporate, statutory bodies, as also the advisory commissions, committees, boards, trusts etc. Affirmative action such as reservations/quotas, including in higher legislative bodies, will be considered whenever necessary on a time-bound basis. Women-friendly personnel policies will also be drawn up to encourage women to participate effectively in the developmental process.

Mainstreaming a Gender Perspective in the Development Process: Policies, programmes and systems would be established to ensure mainstreaming of women's perspectives in all developmental processes, as catalysts, participants and recipients. Wherever there are gaps in policies and programmes, women-specific interventions would be undertaken to bridge these. Coordinating and monitoring mechanisms will also be devised to assess, from time to time, the progress of such mainstreaming mechanisms. Issues and concerns related to women would be specifically addressed and reflected in all concerned laws, sectoral policies, plans and programmes of action.

Economic Empowerment of Women:

Poverty Eradication: Since women comprise the majority of the population below the poverty line and are very often in situations of extreme poverty—given the harsh realities of intra-household and social discrimination—macro economic policies and poverty eradication programmes would specifically address the needs and problems of such women. There would be improved implementation of programmes which are already women-oriented with special targets for women. Steps would be taken for mobilization of poor women and convergence of services, by offering them a range of economic and social options, along with necessary support measures to enhance their capabilities.

Micro Credit: In order to enhance women's access to credit for consumption and production, establishment of new and strengthening of existing micro credit mechanisms and micro-finance institution would be undertaken so that the outreach of credit is enhanced. Other supportive measures would be taken to ensure adequate flow of credit through extant financial institutions and banks so that all women below poverty line have easy access to credit.

Women and Economy: Women's perspectives would be included in designing and implementing macroeconomic and social policies by institutionalizing their participation in such processes. Their contribution to socio-economic development as producers and workers would be recognized in the formal and informal sectors (including home-based workers) and appropriate policies relating to employment and to her working conditions would be drawn up. Such measures could include the following:

1. Reinterpretation and redefinition of conventional concepts of work wherever necessary (e.g. in the census records), to reflect contribution of women as producers and workers.
2. Preparation of satellite and national accounts.
3. Development of appropriate methodologies for undertaking (1) and (2) above.

Globalization: Globalization—the gender impact of which has not been evaluated fully—has presented new challenges for the realization of the goal of women's equality. It is evident that there is a need for re-framing policies for access to employment and quality of employment.

Benefits of the growing global economy have been unevenly distributed leading to wider economic disparities, the feminization of poverty, increased gender inequality through deteriorating working conditions and unsafe working environment especially in the informal economy and rural areas. Strategies would be designed to enhance the capacity of women and empower them to meet the negative social and economic impacts, which may flow from the globalization process.

Women and Agriculture: In view of the critical role of women in the agriculture and allied sectors as producers, concentrated efforts would be made to ensure that benefits of various programmes/schemes reach them in proportion to their numbers. The programmes for training women in soil conservation, social forestry, dairy development and other occupations allied to agriculture (like horticulture, livestock including small animal husbandry, poultry, fisheries etc.) would be expanded to benefit women workers in the agriculture sector.

Women and Industry: The important role played by women in electronics, information technology, food processing, agro industry and textiles has been crucial for the development of these sectors. They would be given comprehensive support in terms of labour legislation, social security and other support services to participate in various industrial sectors.

Women at present cannot work in night shift in factories even if they wish to. Suitable measures will be taken to enable women to work on the night shift in factories. This would be accompanied with support services for security, transportation etc.

Support Services: The provision of support services for women—like child care facilities, including crèches at work places and educational institutions, homes for the aged and the disabled—would be expanded and improved to create an enabling environment and to ensure their full cooperation in social, political and economic life. Women-friendly personnel policies would also be drawn up to encourage women to participate effectively in the developmental process.

Social Empowerment of Women:

Education: Equal access to education for women and girls would be ensured. Special measures would be taken to eliminate discrimination, universalize education, eradicate illiteracy, create a gender-sensitive educational system, increase enrolment and retention rates of girls and improve the quality of education to facilitate life-long learning as well as development of occupation/vocation/technical skills by women. Reducing the gender gap in secondary and higher education would be a focus area. Sectoral time targets in existing policies would be achieved, with a special focus on girls and women, particularly those belonging to weaker sections including the scheduled castes/scheduled tribes/other backward classes/minorities. Gender sensitive curricula would be developed at all levels of educational system in order to address sex stereotyping as one of the causes of gender discrimination.

Health: A holistic approach to women's health which includes both nutrition and health services would be adopted and special attention would be given to the needs of women and the girls at all stages of the life cycle. The reduction of infant mortality and maternal mortality, which are sensitive indicators of human development, is a priority concern. NPEW reiterated the national demographic goals for infant mortality rate (IMR), maternal mortality rate (MMR) set out in the National Population Policy, 2000. Women should have access to comprehensive, affordable and quality health care. Measures would be adopted that take into account the reproductive rights of women to enable them to exercise informed choices, their vulnerability to sexual and health problems together with endemic, infectious and communicable diseases such as malaria, TB, and water borne diseases as well as hypertension and cardio pulmonary diseases. The social, developmental and health consequences of HIV/AIDS and other sexually transmitted diseases would be tackled from a gender perspective.

To effectively meet problems of infant and maternal mortality, and early marriage, the availability of good and accurate data at micro level on deaths, birth and marriages is required. Strict implementation of registration of births and deaths would be ensured and registration of marriages would be made compulsory.

In accordance with the commitment of the National Population Policy, 2000 to population stabilization, NPEW recognized the critical need of men and women to have access to safe, effective and affordable methods of family planning of their choice and the need to suitably address the issues of early marriages and spacing of children. Interventions such as spread of education, compulsory registration of marriage should impact on delaying the age of marriage so that by 2010 child marriages are eliminated.

Women's traditional knowledge about health care and nutrition would be recognized through proper documentation and its use would be encouraged. The use of Indian and alternative systems of medicine would be enhanced within the framework of overall health infrastructure available for women.

Nutrition: In view of the high risk of malnutrition and disease that women face at all the three critical stages, viz. infancy and childhood, adolescent and reproductive phase, focussed attention would be paid to meeting the nutritional needs of women at all stages of the life cycle. This is also important in view of the critical link between the health of adolescent girls, pregnant and lactating women with the health of infant and young children. Special efforts would be made to tackle the problem of macro and micro nutrient deficiencies especially amongst pregnant and lactating women as it leads to various diseases and disabilities.

Intra-household discrimination in nutritional matters vis-à-vis girls and women would be sought to be ended through appropriate strategies. Widespread use of nutrition education would be made to address the issues of intra-household imbalances in nutrition and the special needs of pregnant and lactating women. Women's participation would also be ensured in the planning, superintendence and delivery of the system.

Drinking Water and Sanitation: Special attention would be given to the needs of women in the provision of safe drinking water, sewage disposal, toilet facilities and sanitation within accessible reach of households, especially in rural areas and urban slums. Women's participation would be ensured in the planning, delivery and maintenance of such services.

Housing and Shelter: Women's perspectives would be included in housing policies, planning of housing colonies and provision of shelter both in rural and urban areas. Special attention would be given for providing adequate and safe housing and accommodation for women including single women, heads of households, working women, students, apprentices and trainees.

Environment: Women would be involved and their perspectives reflected in the policies and programmes for environment, conservation and restoration. Considering the impact of environmental factors on their livelihoods, women's participation would be ensured in the conservation of the environment and control of environmental degradation. The vast majority of rural women still depend on the locally available non-commercial sources of energy such as animal dung, crop waste and fuel wood. In order to ensure the efficient use of these energy resources in an environmental friendly manner, NPEW would aim at promoting the programmes of non-conventional energy resources. Women would be involved in spreading the use of solar energy, biogas, smokeless chulahs and other rural application so as to have a visible impact of these measures in influencing eco system and in changing the life styles of rural women.

Science and Technology: Programmes would be strengthened to bring about a greater involvement of women in science and technology. These would include measures to motivate girls to take up science and technology for higher education and also ensure that development projects with scientific and technical inputs involve women fully. Efforts to develop a scientific temper and awareness would also be stepped up. Special measures would be taken for their training in areas where they have special skills like communication and information technology. Efforts to develop appropriate technologies suited to women's needs as well as to reduce their drudgery would be given a special focus too.

Women in Difficult Circumstances: In recognition of the diversity of women's situations and in acknowledgement of the needs of disadvantaged groups, measures and programmes would be undertaken to provide them with special assistance. These groups include women in extreme poverty, destitute women, women in conflict situations, women affected by natural calamities, women in less developed regions, the disabled widows, elderly women, single women in difficult circumstances, women heading households, those displaced from employment, migrants, women who are victims of marital violence, deserted women and prostitutes etc.

Violence against Women: All forms of violence against women, physical and mental, whether at domestic or societal levels, including those arising from customs, traditions or accepted practices shall be dealt with effectively with a view to eliminate its incidence. Institutions and mechanisms for assistance would be created and strengthened for prevention of such violence—including sexual harassment at work place—and for the rehabilitation of the victims of violence and for taking effective action against the perpetrators of such violence. A special emphasis would also be laid on programmes and measures to deal with trafficking in women and girls.

Rights of the Girl Child: All forms of discrimination against the girl child and violation of her rights shall be eliminated by undertaking strong measures both preventive and punitive within and outside the family. These would relate specifically to strict enforcement of laws against pre-natal sex selection and the practices of female foeticide, female infanticide, child marriage, child abuse and child prostitution etc. Removal of discrimination in the treatment of the girl child within the family and outside and projection of a positive image of the girl child would be actively fostered. There would be special emphasis on the needs of the girl child and earmarking of substantial investments in the areas relating to food and nutrition, health and education, and in vocational education. In implementing programmes for eliminating child labour, there would be a special focus on girl children.

Mass Media: Media would be used to portray images consistent with human dignity of girls and women. NPEW would specifically strive to remove demeaning, degrading and negative conventional stereotypical images of women and violence against women. Private sector partners and media networks would be involved at all levels to ensure equal access for women, particularly in the area of information and communication technologies. The media would be encouraged to develop codes of conduct, professional guidelines and other self-regulatory mechanisms to remove gender stereotypes and promote balanced portrayals of women and men.

Operational Strategies of NPEW

Action Plans: All Central and State Ministries would draw up time bound Action Plans for translating NPEW into a set of concrete actions, through a participatory process of consultation with Central/State Departments of Women and Child Development and National/State Commissions for Women. The Plans would specifically include the following:

1. Measurable goals to be achieved by 2010.
2. Identification and commitment of resources.
3. Responsibilities for implementation of action points.
4. Structures and mechanisms to ensure efficient monitoring, review and gender impact assessment of action points and policies.
5. Introduction of a gender perspective in the budgeting process.

In order to support better planning and programme formulation and adequate allocation of resources, gender development indices (GDI) would be developed by networking with specialized agencies. These could be analyzed and studied in depth. Gender auditing and development of evaluation mechanisms would also be undertaken along side.

Collection of gender disaggregated data by all primary data collecting agencies of the Central and State Governments as well as research and academic institutions in the public and private sectors would be undertaken. Data and information gaps in vital areas reflecting the status of women would be sought to be filled in by these immediately. All Ministries/corporations/banks and financial institutions etc. would be advised to collect, collate, disseminate and maintain/publish data related to programmes and benefits on a gender disaggregated basis. This would help in meaningful planning and evaluation of policies.

Institutional Mechanisms: Institutional mechanisms, to promote the advancement of women, which exist at the Central and State levels, would be strengthened. This would be done through appropriate and would relate to, among others, provision of adequate resources, training and skills to effectively influence macro policies, legislations, programmes etc. to achieve the empowerment of women.

National and State Councils would be formed to oversee the operationalisation of the Policy on a regular basis. The National Council would be headed by the Prime Minister and the State Councils by the Chief Ministers and would be broad in composition having representatives from the concerned Departments/Ministries, National and State Commissions for Women, Social Welfare Boards, representatives of non-government organizations, women's organisations, corporate sector, trade unions, financing institutions, academics, experts and social activists. These bodies would review the progress made in implementing the Policy twice a year. The National Development Council would also be informed, from time to time, of the progress of the programme undertaken under the policy for advice and comments.

National and State Resource Centres on women would be

established with mandates for collection and dissemination of information, undertaking research work, conducting surveys, implementing training and awareness generation programmes etc. These centres would link up with women's studies centres and other research and academic institutions through suitable information networking systems.

While institutions at the district level would be strengthened, women would be helped by Government at the grassroots level through its programmes to organize and strengthen self-help groups (SHGs) at the anganwadi/village/town levels. The women's groups would be helped to institutionalize themselves into registered societies and to federate at the panchyat/municipal level. These societies would bring about synergistic implementation of all the social and economic development programmes by drawing resources made available through Government and non-government channels, including banks and financial institutions and by establishing a close interface with the panchayats/municipalities.

Resource Management: Availability of adequate financial, human and market resources to implement NPEW would be managed by concerned departments, financial credit institutions and banks, private sector, civil society and other connected institutions. This process would include the following:

1. Assessment of benefits flowing to women and resource allocation to the programmes relating to them through an exercise of gender budgeting. Appropriate changes in policies would be made to optimize benefits to women under these schemes.
2. Adequate resource allocation to develop and promote the policy outlined earlier based on (1) above by concerned Departments.
3. Developing synergy between personnel of health, rural development, education and women and child development department at field level and other village level functionaries.
4. Meeting credit needs by banks and financial credit

institutions through suitable policy initiatives and development of new institutions in coordination with the Department of Women and Child Development.

The strategy of Women's Component Plan adopted in the Ninth Five Year Plan (1997-98 to 2001-02) ensuring that not less than 30 percent of benefits/funds flow to women from all Ministries and Departments would be implemented effectively so that the needs and interests of women and girls are addressed by all concerned sectors. The Department of Women and Child Development being the nodal Ministry will monitor and review the progress of the implementation of the Component Plan from time to time in terms of both quality and quantity in collaboration with the Planning Commission.

Efforts would be made to channelize private sector investments also, to support programmes and projects for advancement of women.

Legislation: The existing legislative structure would be reviewed and additional legislative measures taken by identified departments to implement the Policy. This would also involve a review of all existing laws including personal, customary and tribal laws, subordinate legislation, related rules as well as executive and administrative regulations to eliminate all gender discriminatory references. The process would be planned over a time period 2000-2003. The specific measures required would be evolved through a consultation process involving civil society, National Commission for Women, and Department of Women and Child Development. In appropriate cases the consultation process would be widened to include other stakeholders also.

Effective implementation of legislations would be promoted by involving civil society and community. Appropriate changes in legislations would be undertaken, if necessary. In addition, following other specific measures would be taken to implement the legislation effectively:

1. Strict enforcement of all relevant legal provisions and speedy redressal of grievances would be ensured, with a

special focus on violence and gender related atrocities.

2. Measures to prevent and punish sexual harassment at the place of work, protection for women workers in the organized/unorganized sector and strict enforcement of relevant laws such as Equal Remuneration Act and Minimum Wages Act would be undertaken.
3. Crimes against women, their incidence, prevention, investigation, detection and prosecution would be regularly reviewed at all crime review fora and conferences at the Central, State and District levels. Recognised, local, voluntary organizations would be authorized to lodge complaints and facilitate registration, investigations and legal proceedings related to violence and atrocities against girls and women.
4. Women's cells in police stations, women police stations, family courts, mahila courts, counselling centres, legal aid centres and nyaya panchayats would be strengthened and expanded to eliminate violence and atrocities against women.
5. Widespread dissemination of information on all aspects of legal rights, human rights and other entitlements of women, through specially designed legal literacy programmes and rights information programmes would be done.

Gender Sensitization: Training of personnel of executive, legislative and judicial wings of the State—with a special focus on policy and programme framers, implementation and development agencies, law enforcement machinery and the judiciary, as well as non-governmental organizations—would be undertaken. Other measures would include the following:

1. Promoting societal awareness of gender issues and women's human rights.
2. Review of curriculum and educational materials to include gender education and human rights issues.
3. Removal of all references derogatory to the dignity of women from all public documents and legal instruments.
4. Use of different forms of mass media to communicate social messages relating to women's equality and empowerment.

Panchayati Raj Institutions: The 73rd and 74th Amendments to the Indian Constitution have served as a breakthrough towards ensuring equal access and increased participation of women in political power structure. The PRIs would play a central role in the process of enhancing women's participation in public life. The PRIs and the local self-governments would be actively involved in the implementation and execution of NPEW the grassroots level.

Partnership with the Voluntary Sector Organizations: The involvement of voluntary organizations, associations, federations, trade unions, non-governmental organizations, women's organizations, as well as institutions dealing with education, training and research would be ensured in the formulation, implementation, monitoring and review of all policies and programmes affecting women. Towards this end, they would be provided with appropriate support related to resources and capacity building and facilitated to participate actively in the process of the empowerment of women.

International Cooperation: NPEW would aim at implementation of international obligations/commitments in all sectors on empowerment of women such as the Convention on All Forms of Discrimination against Women (CEDAW), Convention on the Rights of the Child (CRC), International Conference on Population and Development (ICPD) and other such instruments. International, regional and sub-regional cooperation towards the empowerment of women would continue to be encouraged through sharing of experiences, exchange of ideas and technology, networking with institutions and organizations and through bilateral and multi-lateral partnerships.

Bibliography

Bibliography

Ahmad, Z. (2011), "Evidence of the Characteristics of Women Entrepreneurs in the Kingdom of Saudi Arabia: An Empirical Investigation", *International Journal of Gender and Entrepreneurship*, 3(2), 123-143.

Ali, A. and Haider, J. (2012), "Impact of Internal Organizational Communications on Employee Job Satisfaction: Case of Some Pakistani Banks", *Global Advanced Research Journal of Management and Business Studies*, 1(10), 38-44.

Almer, E.D. and Kaplan, S.E. (2002), "The Effects of Flexible Work Arrangements on Stressors, Burnout and Behavioural Job Outcomes in Public Accounting", *Behavioural Research in Accounting*, 14(1), 1-34.

Altintas, F. and Altintas, M. (2008), "The Relationship between Feminist/Womanist Identity and Leadership Styles of Women Managers in Turkey", *Gender in Management: An International Journal*, 23(3), 175-193.

Amondi, O.B. (2011), "Representation of Women in Top Educational Management and Leadership Positions in Kenya", *Advancing Women in Leadership*, 31, 57-62.

Asgari, A., Silong, A.D., Ahmad, A. and Sama, B.A. (2008), "The Relationship between Transformational Leadership Behaviours, Leader-Member Exchange and Organizational Citizenship Behaviours", *European Journal of Social Sciences*, 6(4), 140-151.

Ashmos, D.P., Duchon, D., McDaniel, R.R. and Huonker, J.W. (2002), "What a Mess! Participation as a Simple Managerial Rule to Complexity Organisations", *Journal of Management Studies*, 39(2), 189-206.

Barrett, D. (2006), "Leadership Communication: A Communication Approach for Senior-Level Managers", *Handbook of Business Strategy*, 21(1), 385-390.

Bass, B. (1988), "The Inspirational Processes of Leadership", *Journal of Management Development*, 7(5), 21-31.

Bateh, J. and Heyliger, W. (2014), "Academic Administrator Leadership Styles and the Impact of Faculty Job Satisfaction", *Journal of Leadership Education*, 3(2), 22-32.

Bentler, P.M. and Bonnet, D.C. (1980), "Significance Tests and Goodness of Fit in the Analysis of Covariance Structures", *Psychological Bulletin*, 88(3), 588-606.

Beri, G.C. (2005), "Marketing Research", 3rd edition, New Delhi: Tata McGraw-Hill.

Biradar, R.R. (2005), "Incidence of Poverty Among Social Groups in Rural India: Why Do SCs/STs Experience Greater Incidence of Poverty', Paper Presented at the Foundation-Day Seminar, National Institute for Rural Development (NIRD), Hyderabad, held during November 9-10, 2005.

Cano, J. and Castillo, J.X. (2004), Factors Explaining Job Satisfaction among Faculty", *Journal of Agricultural Education*, 45(3), 65-74.

Chadha, G.K. and Sharma, Alakh N. (eds.) (1997), "Growth, Employment and Poverty: Change and Continuity in Rural India", Vikas Publishing House Pvt. Ltd., New Delhi.

Chakraborty, S. and Sengupta, K. (2014), "Structural Equation Modelling of Determinants of Customer Satisfaction of Mobile Network Providers: Case of Kolkata", *IIMB Management Review*, 26(4), 234-248.

Chaudhry, A.Q. and Javed, H. (2012), "Impact of Transactional and Laissez Faire Leadership Style on Motivation", *International Journal of Business and Social Science*, 3(7), 258-264.

Chughtai, A.A. and Zafar, S. (2006), "Antecedents and Consequences of Organisational Commitment among Pakistani University Teachers", *Leadership Quarterly*, 3(3), 111-121.

Deaton, A. and Dreze, Jean (2002), "Poverty and Inequality in India: A Re-examination", *Economic and Political Weekly*, September 7.

Dreze, J and Srinivasan, P.V. (1997), "Widowhood and Poverty in Rural India: Some Inferences from Household Survey Data", *Journal of Development Economics*, 54(2) 217-234.

Dreze, Jean and Sen, A. (2002), "India: Development and Participation", Oxford University Press, New Delhi.

Dreze, Jean and Sen, A. (1995), "Indian Economic Development and Social Opportunity", Oxford University Press, New Delhi.

Dutta, B. and Ramaswami, B. (2001), "Targeting and Efficiency in the Public Distribution System", *Economic and Political Weekly*, Volume 36, May.

Eagly, A.H. and Johannesen, M.C. (2001), "The Leadership Styles of

Women and Men", *Journal of Social Issues*, 57(4), 781-797.

Evans, D. (2010), "Aspiring to Leadership: A Woman's World? An Example of Developments in France", *Cross Cultural Management: An International Journal*, 17(4), 347-367.

Fan, Shenggen, Hazell, Peter B.R. and Thorat, Sukhadeo (2000), "Government Spending, Growth and Poverty in Rural India", *American Journal of Agricultural Economics*, 82(4), 1038-1051.

Fernandes, C. and Awamleh, R. (2011), "The Impact of Transformational and Transactional Leadership Styles on Employees' Satisfaction and Performance: An Empirical Test in a Multicultural Environment", *International Business and Economics Research Journal*, 3(8), 1-16.

Field, A. (2009), "Discovering Statistics Using SPSS", Sage Publications.

Fisher, Thomas and Sriram, M.S. (2000), "Beyond Micro-credit: Putting Development Back into Micro-finance", Vistaar Publications, New Delhi.

Gabillon, Z. (2005), "Learner's Beliefs: An Overview", *Journal of Language and Learning*, 3(2), 233-260.

George, N. and Kicku, J. (2000), "Emergent Leadership Behaviours: The Function of Personality and Cognitive Ability in Determining Teamwork Performance", *Journal of Business and Psychology,* 15(1), 27-51.

Giri, R. and Das, A.K. (2011), "Indian Citation Index: A New Web Platform for Measuring Performance of Indian Research Periodicals", *Library Hi Tech News*, 28(3), 33-35.

Greening, H. and Randhwa, Bikki (1999), "A Framework for Regulating Microfinance Institutions", The World Bank.

Haider, M.H. and Riaz, A. (2010), "Role of Transformational and Transactional Leadership with Job Satisfaction and Career Satisfaction", *Business and Economic Horizons*, 12(1), 29-38.

Harris, C.A. and Leberman, S.I. (2011), "Leadership Development for Women in New Zealand Universities: Learning From the New Zealand Women in Leadership Program", *Advances in Developing Human Resources*, 15(2), 22-32.

Hartog, J., Ferrer, A. and Jonker, N. (2002), "Linking Measured Risk Aversion to Individual Characteristics", *Kyklos*, 55(1), 3-26.

Hassan, Z., and Silong, A.D. (2008), "Women Leadership and Community Development", *European Journal of Scientific Research*, 23(3), 361-372.

Hirway, Indira (1986), "Wage Employment Programmes in Rural Development", Oxford and IBH Publishing Co. Pvt. Ltd., New Delhi.

Hopkins, M.M., O'Neil, D.A. and Bilimoria, D. (2006), "Effective Leadership and Successful Career Advancement: Perspectives from Women in Healthcare", *Equal Opportunities International*, 25(4), 251-271.

Hunjra, A.I., Chani, M.I., Aslam, S., Azam, M. and Rehman, K.U. (2010), "Factors Effecting Job Satisfaction of Employees in Pakistani Banking Sector", *African Journal of Business Management*, 4(10), 2157-2163.

Iqbal, N., Anwar, S. and Haider, N. (2015), "Effect of Leadership Style on Employee Performance", *Arabian Journal of Business and Management Review*, 20(5), 6-14.

Islam, J., Mohajan, H. and Datta, R. (2011), "A Study on Job Satisfaction and Morale of Commercial Banks in Bangladesh", *Review of Applied Socio-economic Research*, 4(2), 33-46.

Jogulu, U.D. and Wood, G.J. (2006), "The Role of Leadership Theory in Raising the Profile of Women in Management", *Equal Opportunities International*, 25(4), 236-250.

Joshi, Sandeep (2000), "Panchayati Raj Institutions and Poverty Alleviation", Rawat Publications, Jaipur.

Karimi, L. (2008), "A Study of a Multidimensional Model of Work-Family Conflict among Iranian Employees", *Community, Work and Family*, 11(3), 283-295.

Kaur, R. (2012), "Transformational and Transactional Leadership Behaviour in Selected Public and Private Sector Banks in Chandigarh", *International Journal of Engineering and Management Sciences*, 3(2), 126-133.

Khan, M.M., Ramzan, M., Ahmed, I. and Nawaz, M. (2011), "Transformational, Transactional and Laissez Faire Styles of Teaching Faculty as Predictors of Satisfaction and Extra Effort among the Students: Evidence from Higher Education Institutions", *Interdisciplinary Journal of Research in Business*, 1(4), 130-135.

Kiboss, J.K., and Jemiryott, H.K. (2014), "Relationship between Principals' Leadership Styles and Secondary School Teachers' Job Satisfaction in Nandi South District, Kenya", *Journal of Education and Human Development*, 3(2), 493-509.

Klaauw, B.V. and Limin Wang (2004), "Child Mortality in Rural

India", World Bank, Washington, D.C.

Lyons, J.B. and Schneider, T.R. (2009), "The Effects of Leadership Style on Stress Outcomes", *The Leadership Quarterly*, 20(5), 737-748.

Malhotra, D. (2004), "Trust and Reciprocity Decisions: The Differing Perspectives of Trustees and Trusted Parties", *Organisational Behaviour and Human Decision Processes*, 94(2), 61-73.

Malik, S.H., Aziz, S. and Hassan, H. (2014), Leadership Behaviour and Acceptance of Leaders by Subordinates: Application of Path Goal Theory in Telecom Sector", *International Journal of Trade, Economics and Finance*, 5(2), 170-186.

Mansoor, M., and Bilal, R.U. (2012), "The Impact of Leadership Styles on Job Satisfaction at Work Place", *Arabian Journal of Business and Management Review,* 1(12), 26.

Mehta, R., Dubinsky, A.J. and Anderson, R.E. (2003), "Leadership Style, Motivation and Performance in International Marketing Channels: An Empirical Investigation of USA, Finland and Poland", *European Journal of Marketing*, 37(1), 50-85.

Minhas. B.S., Jain, L.R. and Tendulkar, S.D. (1991), "Declining Incidence of Poverty in the 1980s: Evidence vs. Artefacts", *Economic and Political Weekly,* Volume 26, July 6-13.

Mishra, P.S. and Mohapatra, A.D. (2010), "Relevance of Emotional Intelligence for Effective Job Performance: An Empirical Study", *Vikalpa*, 35(1), 53-61.

Moran, B.B. (1992), "Gender Differences in Leadership", *Library Trends*, 40(3), 475-491.

Narasimhan, Sankuntala (1999), "Empowering Women: An Alternative Strategy from Rural India", Sage Publications, New Delhi.

Nayyar, P., Sharma, A., Kishtwaria, J., Rana, A. and Vyas, N. (2007), "Causes and Constraints Faced by Women Entrepreneurs in Entrepreneurial Process", *The Journal of Social Science*, 14(2), 99-102.

Oguz, E. (2010), "The Relationship between the Leadership Styles of the School Administrators and the Organisational Citizenship Behaviours of Teachers", *Procedia-Social and Behavioural Sciences*, 9, 1188-1193.

Omar, W. and Hussain, F. (2013), "Transformational Leadership Style and Job Satisfaction Relationship: A Study of Structural

Equation Modelling (SEM)", *International Journal of Academic Research in Business and Social sciences*, 3(2), 346.

Panchmukhi, V.R. and Brahamananda, P. (1987), "Development Process of the Indian Economy", Bombay: Himalaya Publishing House.

Paracha, M.U., Qamar, A., Mirza, A., Hassan, I. and Waqas, H. (2012), "Impact of Leadership Style (Transformational and Transactional Leadership) on Employee Performance and Mediating Role of Job Satisfaction: A Study of Private School in Pakistan", *Global Journal of Management and Business Research*, 12(4), 54-64.

Patnaik, Prabhat (2005), "On the Need for Providing Employment Guarantee", *Economic and Political Weekly,* January.

Pradeep, D.D. and Prabhu, N.R.V. (2011), "The Relationship between Effective Leadership and Employee Performance", *Journal of Advancements in Information Technology*, 20, 198-207.

Purushothaman, Sangeetha (1998), "The Empowerment of Women in India: Grassroots Women's Networks and State", Sage Publications, New Delhi.

Radhakrishna, R., Rao, K. Hanumantha, Ravi, C., Reddy, B. Sambi (2004), "Chronic Poverty and Malnutrition in 1990s", *Economic and Political Weekly,* July 10.

Rajasekhar, D. (2000), "Non-government Organizations (NGOs) in India: Opportunities and Challenges", *Journal of Rural Development*, Volume 19, No. 2.

Ram, P. and Prabhakar, G.V. (2010), Leadership Styles and Perceived Organizational Politics as Predictors of Work Related Outcomes", *European Journal of Social Sciences*, 15(1), 40-55.

Raman, K., Anantharaman, R.N. and Jayasingam, S. (2008), "Motivational Factors Affecting Entrepreneurial Decision: A Comparison between Malaysian Women Entrepreneurs and Women Non-Entrepreneurs", *Communications of the IBIMA*, 2(12), 85-89.

Ravallion, Martin (2000), "What is Needed for a More Pro-Poor Growth Process in India", *Economic and Political Weekly*, Volume 35, March 25-31.

Ray, R. (2000), "Poverty, Household Size and Child Welfare in India", *Economic and Political Weekly*, September 23.

Subramanian, S. (2011), "Inclusive Development and the Quintile Income Statistic", *Economic and Political Weekly,* Volume 46,

January 22.

Saleem, S., Majeedand, S. and Aziz, T. (2013), "Determinants of Job Satisfaction among Employees of Banking Industry at Bahawalpur", *Journal of Emerging Issues in Economics, Finance and Banking*, 1(2), 150-162.

Sandhya, K. and Kumar, D.P. (2011), "Employee Retention by Motivation", *Indian Journal of Science and Technology*, 4(12), 1778-1782.

Sinha, Saurabh (1998), "Micro Credit: Impact, Training and Sustainability", Institute of Development Studies (IDS), Volume 29, No. 4, October, University Sussex, U.K.

Shetty, S.L. (2003), "Credit Flows to Rural Poor", mimeo, EPW Research Foundation, Mumbai.

Shusha, A. (2013), "The Mediating Role of Leader-Member Exchange in the Relationship between Transformational Leadership and Job Performance", *European Journal of Business and Management*, 5(8), 157-164.

Singh, N., and Krishnan, V.R. (2008), "Self-sacrifice and Transformational Leadership: Mediating Role of Altruism", *Leadership and Organization Development Journal*, 29(3), 261-274.

Stern, Nicholas H. (2001), "Building a Climate for Investment, Growth and Poverty Reduction in India", 16th Exim Bank Commencement Day Annual Lecture, Mumbai.

Talukhaba, A., Mutunga, T. and Miruka, C.O. (2011), "Indicators of Effective Communication Models in Remote Projects", *International Journal of Project Organisation and Management*, 3(2), 127-138.

Thorat, Sukhadeo (2004), "Persistence of Poverty: Why do Scheduled Castes and Scheduled Tribes Stay Chronically Poor?", Working Paper for Centre for Chronic Poverty, London.

Tipu, S.A. and Ryan, J.C. (2011), "Communication, Commitment and Trust: Exploring the Triad", *International Journal of Business and Management*, 6(6), 77-83.

Vijay Mahajan (2005), "Micro Finance to Livelihood Finance", *Economic and Political Weekly*, Volume XL, No. 41.

Viswanath, Vanita (1993), "NGOs and Women's Development in Rural South India: A Comparative Analysis", Vistaar Publications, New Delhi.

Wright, B.E. and Pandey, S.K. (2009), "Transformational Leadership in the Public Sector: Does Structure Matter?", *Journal of Public Administration Research and Theory*, 3(1), 10-22.

Yaseen, Z. (2010), "Leadership Styles of Men and Women in the Arab World", *Education, Business and Society: Contemporary Middle Eastern Issues*, 3(1), 63-70.

Yunus, N.J. and Anuar, S. (2012), "Trust as Moderating Effect between Emotional Intelligence and Leadership Styles", *Interdisciplinary Journal of Contemporary Research in Business*, 3(10), 650-663.

Zaccaro, S.J., Rittman, A.L. and Marks, M.A. (2002), "Team Leadership", *The Leadership Quarterly*, 12(4), 451-483.

Websites

Ministry of Women and Child Development
Ministry of Social Justice and Empowerment
Ministry of Panchayati Raj

Index

Index